BASEBALL IN FORT WORTH

BASEBALL IN FORT WORTH

Mark Presswood and Chris Holaday

ARCADIA
PUBLISHING

Published by Arcadia Publishing
Charleston, South Carolina

Library of Congress Catalog Card Number: 2004100872

For all general information contact Arcadia Publishing at:
Telephone 843-853-2070
Fax 843-853-0044
E-Mail sales@arcadiapublishing.com
For customer service and orders:
Toll-Free 1-888-313-2665

Visit us on the Internet at www.arcadiapublishing.com

This book is dedicated to all of the hard working staffs of minor league baseball teams whose front office efforts are rarely recognized but are such an important part of the game. From Marketing to Ticket Sales, Promotions and Advertising their work behind the field of dreams make it possible for all of us to enjoy the action on the field.

Mark would like to especially recognize the wonderful Cats' staff members that since their return have focused on making the fan experience their number one priority. If we left someone out we apologize in advance but your efforts are not forgotten. To Monty Clegg, Michael Halbrooks, Scott Berry, Tim Sims, Brant Ringler, Stan Allen, Sherri Gutkowski, David Boyd, Pat Fulps, Carter Wooten, Jared Moise, Ryan Fergus, Mike Barron, John Bilbow, Jeff Carman, Candiss Caudle, Stacy Navarro, Kyle Smith and wife Carla, Sunni Watson, Cynthia Ward, Shayne Forsyth, Kevin Forrester, Mike Tidwell, Jennifer and Angela Spidell, and the many other interns and volunteers we thank you for all you do.

Most importantly Mark would like to thank his wife, Pam, and the kids Trey, Alyssa, and Bret for all of their love, support, and allowing him to participate in the National Pastime.

CONTENTS

ACKNOWLEDGMENTS

A great deal of gratitude goes to the following people and organizations for their assistance in compiling and writing this book.

Max Hill & the Fort Worth Public Library, for great assistance for our research and access to their archives; David Hatchett & Emil Moffatt—Fort Worth Cats staff—for access and collection of current Fort Worth baseball photos; William Blair—former Negro League baseball player—for conversations on Fort Worth's black Baseball History; Cory Tucker—Coach, Teacher, and Father—for his wonderful collection of photos from the 1930s; Jim Noah—Fort Worth Firefighter historian—for his wonderful collection of Fort Worth's Firefighters History; John Esch—baseball card collector & Bobby Bragan Youth Foundation President—for his wonderful baseball card and postcard collection; James Jasek—Waco historian and printer—for his wonderful collection of Waco photos; UTA Special Collections & the *Fort Worth Star-Telegram Newspaper*, for access to the 1905 Panthers photo; Marion Jones—coach, teacher, and world class athlete—for sharing the history of Fort Worth's black baseball history; Robert Phelan—grandson of former Panther Arthur 'Dugan' Phelan—for a great photo collection of the 1920s Panthers; Jeff Guinn—books editor for the *Star Telegram*—whose inspirational book *When Panthers Roared* made this easier; Nora Townsend—daughter of Mo Santomauro—for Photos of her Dad; Carroll Beringer, Jack Lindsey, and Mike Napoli—former Cats players—for their great recollections and photos of Fort Worth's baseball past; Jay Black and the Texas Sports Hall of Fame in Waco. Jeff Ruetsche—our Arcadia Publishing editor—for his patience and belief in this project.

INTRODUCTION

The first mention of baseball in Fort Worth is an 1877 newspaper article describing the events on April 5th when a team from Texarkana came to town to "play the local nine on the level prairie south of town." Though no account of the game could be found, an article from April 20th of the same year had the Fort Worth nine beating Dallas, 17-12. It was also the first mention that the team had adopted the nickname Panthers. During this time Dallas and Fort Worth were vying for commerce and business growth in a difficult economic period. Mud slinging between newspapers from the two cities led to a Dallas newspaper article claiming, "Fort Worth is so sleepy a Panther can be found sleeping on the town square." Instead of fighting back in newsprint the town adopted the Panther mascot and became known as Panther City.

For many years, Fort Worth served as the gathering point for cattle herds being shipped to the northern meat packing plants and the north Fort Worth stockyards provided a last stop before being loaded on trains. The rowdy bands of cowboys, driving herds to Fort Worth, worked hard and played harder, finding entertainment in the raucous part of downtown known as "Hell's Half Acre." Eventually packing companies were built on the north side to prepare the cattle in Fort Worth with the Swift Armour Company building the largest facility and becoming the biggest employer in 1903. Rogers Hornsby, later one of major leagues baseball's most famous stars, moved with his family to Fort Worth when they chose to work in the meat packing plants.

Samuel Hain from Houston is credited with starting the first semblance of an organized baseball league in Texas. Houston, Galveston, San Antonio, Waco, Dallas, and Fort Worth were represented, but this was by no means a professional league. One account had a Fort Worth team traveling to Houston for a game by buckboard, taking over a week to make the journey. Professional teams from the north also began barnstorming in Texas and an 1887 game between the St. Louis Browns and an All-Star group of National League players is recognized as the first all professional game played in the state. A short time later, John McCloskey brought his professional Joplin team into Texas and played both Fort Worth and Dallas amateur teams. McCloskey, enamored with the excitement of the games, became the father of the state's first professional circuit when he helped organized the Texas League of Professional Baseball Clubs in 1888.

Though financially unstable through the early years, both the Texas League and Fort Worth managed to put on baseball games for the fans in most years. The African-American communities also began organizing teams and playing games with teams from other cities and towns. Though no formal professional league existed for black players until much later there were many "rousing occasions of ball being played." As transportation around the state became less difficult the Texas League was able to stabilize. Fort Worth would play host to teams representing Texas League cities from the southern part of the state as well as Oklahoma and Louisiana. No guest was more anticipated, however, than the baseball nine from neighboring Dallas.

The playing fields in Fort Worth moved from the south side of downtown to the near north side, just over the Trinity River bluffs. As the population grew so did the fan capacity of these fields. The first held 1,200 fans, the last 13,000, and the current around 8,000. The Panthers eventually became one of the most famous minor league teams in history, winning six straight Texas League Championships during the 1920s. Play continued through the Depression with the Panthers winning championships at the beginning and end of the '30s decade. After a pause for World War II, professional baseball in Fort Worth was resurrected when the city's franchise was purchased by the Brooklyn Dodgers. Many famous future Dodgers of the 1950s played their way to the majors through Fort Worth. It all ended with the team's merger with Dallas and when play moved to Arlington and Turnpike Stadium as the Dallas-Fort Worth Spurs in 1965.

Fort Worth has grown from its Panther City roots to its current 'Cowtown' nickname and a very proud western heritage. Fort Worth plays host to one of the largest Fat Stock Shows in the country and is now home to the National Cowgirl Museum and Hall of Fame and the world's oldest indoor rodeo. In addition, the city is known for the arts with the Amon Carter Museum, the Modern Art Museum of Fort Worth and the world-renown Kimbell Museum of Art all calling Fort Worth home. Professional baseball has also returned, presented every May through August at the historic LaGrave Field site by the new Fort Worth Cats.

Fort Worth's new LaGrave Field, built on the site where baseball has been played in the city since the 1920s, was recently featured in *Baseball America*'s ballpark calendar and voted by the same publication as one of the best independent league ballparks in the nation.

ONE

The Prarie Grows
1888–1918

The history of professional baseball in Texas has been well chronicled in several past and recent publications. The Texas League of Professional Baseball Clubs has served as the foundation and organization for professional baseball in Texas for almost one hundred and twenty years. The birth of the circuit began when teams from the Texas cities of Austin, Dallas, Galveston, San Antonio, and Fort Worth, as well as New Orleans, Louisiana, took to the field for the state's first schedule of professional games on April 8, 1888. The league was not stable and well organized, and financial troubles, rule violations, players disregarding contracts, and failure to play several seasons marred the early years of the league.

For reasons that were primarily financial, the Texas League failed to operate in 1891,1893,1894,1900, and 1901 and for these five years Fort Worth did not field a team. The Spanish-American War helped derail the league in 1898 as many players, especially in Texas, went off to war. The Panthers started that season but played only nineteen games before disbanding.

Many teams throughout this era failed to generate the revenues needed to pay bills and players and thus ceased operations. Ardmore, Denison, Paris, Cleburne, Temple, and Texarkana were a few of the teams that entered and exited the league after very short tenures. Corsicana fielded teams from 1902 through 1905 and won two championships, but the club could not meet the financial commitments, and folded. In Fort Worth, behind the efforts of owner William H. Ward and another stock ownership group that included at different times John Cella, W.B. Elliott, and Newton H. Lassiter, the Panthers were kept alive and financially sound when the league existed.

Starting with the 1907 season the Texas League re-formed to include an all-Texas contingent of teams. The South Texas league had operated as a separate organization from 1898 through the 1906 season but came together with the cities in the northern part of the state to form what some recognize as the true start of the Texas League in 1907. Except for Shreveport and Austin switching franchises twice, this era of the Texas League was stable and strong into World War I. Fort Worth's entries had varied success in those early years but were recognized as league champions for the 1895 and 1905 seasons. The club had won first half titles in 1896 and 1906 but both times failed to field a team for the second half (1896) or playoffs (1906) after disbanding.

Housing developments, skyscrapers, and concrete have replaced the prairie of this late 1800s postcard, but Fort Worth will forever be linked to its western heritage and cowboy toughness. The early accounts of baseball in Fort Worth refer to the team playing on "the level prairie south of town." Currently this area of Fort Worth is just north of the hospital district and covered with stately oaks and other large trees among the houses and businesses. Obviously, as this early photo indicates, the trees were not native to the landscape.

The Panthers first entry in 1888 included several well known "baseballists" of the time including Art Sunday, Texas League co-founder "Big" Mike O'Connor, Emmet Rogers and William "Farmer" Works. William "Scrappy" Joyce also played for the 1888 Panthers and is recognized as the first Texas League alumnus to manage a major league club (New York Giants). It was still another William who is recognized as the first Fort Worth native to play in the major leagues. William "Doc" Nance was born in August of 1876 and went on to a three-year major league career with Louisville and the Detroit Tigers. In this photo Nance is shown when he coached Texas Christian University's baseball team in the early 1920s.

Many early town teams were nothing more than local laborers who had either played during their military service or had watched a game. This 1888 photo of a team from Odessa, Texas shows the kind of competition available to Fort Worth town teams prior to the start of the more organized professional leagues. Uniforms and equipment were not readily available at the time. The caption on the back identifies the young man kneeling on far left of the front row and holding a baseball as Frank Royster.

The 1895 Texas League Champion Fort Worth Panthers won the first professional sport championship for Fort Worth. To boost attendance for second-tier teams the league office decided to declare a first half champion and then crown a second half champion, which would lead to a playoff at season's end. Dallas was declared the first half champion and Fort Worth won the second half. A fifteen-game series was agreed to by both owners, but after Fort Worth had taken a seven games to six lead, rain and an argument over where the next two games were to be played led to a discontinued series. Fort Worth was declared champions during the league meetings the following January. Pitcher Alex McFarland led the team and set the still-standing league record of 34 wins. Sport McAllister and Jack Jarvis were also tough on the hill.

The offense on the 1895 team was led by future big leaguer Harry Steinfeldt. Steinfeldt was a major force on the winning Chicago Cubs teams from 1906 to 1910, but is best remembered as the third baseman left out of the famous Franklin P. Adams's poem of 1910 entitled "Baseball's Sad Lexicon." The poem refers to the famous Chicago Cubs double play combination of "Tinker to Evers to Chance." While with the Panthers Steinfeldt was primarily a second baseman and he led the league in fielding percentage in 1896, splitting the season between Fort Worth and Galveston.

This 1904 Panthers team had the best overall record (72-30) in the league and won the second half title by twelve games over Dallas. Fort Worth met first half champion Corsicana, whose team was bolstered by Dallas players, in a nineteen game playoff format. Corsicana won eleven to Fort Worth's eight and was declared champion. Jack Jarvis, Charlie Jackson (26 wins), and Harold Chrisman (21 wins) led the pitching staff while future University of Texas coach William "Billy" Disch, George Reitz, Lew Haidt, catcher Hugh McMurray, and outfielder Dee Poindexter led the hitters.

William "Jack" "Red" Jarvis pitched for the Panthers in 1895, 1898, 1902, 1903, and parts of the 1904 and 1906 seasons. Jarvis led the league in strikeouts in 1904 with 185 helping the team to a first place finish during the regular season before the Panthers lost to Corsicana in the League Championship series. He also helped the Panthers win their first championship in 1895. He won 20 games in 1908 while pitching for Houston. Jarvis is one of the many former players who chose to find a home and a new profession in Fort Worth after their playing career was over.

The 1905 San Antonio Bronchos featured three players that would have a major impact on baseball in both Texas and Fort Worth over the next thirty years. J. Walter Morris (center) purchased the Fort Worth Club in the winter of 1909 and served as the team's manager from 1910 through the beginning of the 1913 season. He became Texas League President in 1916 and would also serve as President of three other minor leagues. Tony Thebo (right) was a fleet footed centerfielder for eleven Texas League seasons and was a constant source of information for Paul LaGrave (left). The relationship LaGrave built with Morris helped him secure a front office position both when Morris took over the Panthers and when as league President Morris recommended him for the Business Manager role to W. K. Stripling.

Top Row: D. Cavendor L.F.- Leo. Walsh P.- Mike Erwin C.- Owen Wilson R.F.- Ed. Hanlon P.- Ed. Wieker P.
Middle Row: Ridy Schenwinek P.- Tom Huddleston P.- Heavy Wills 1st B.- Ollie Gfroeren C.F.
Bottom Row: Bob Christman P.- Pat Maugh C.- George Markay 3rd B.- Walter Boles. SS.- A. Pennell 2nd B.

1905 PENNANT WINNERS.

The 1905 team was the second championship team in Fort Worth's history. The Panthers were four games behind the league-leading Temple Boll Weevils with six games to play. The Panthers swept a four game series with Temple then, while Temple was splitting a series with Dallas, the Panthers swept Waco to take the Texas League Championship. The league played on Sundays for the first time that season after a court case involving the Waco club allowed for the games. Harold Chrisman (bottom row, second from left) had a 23-14 record with 218 strikeouts. He also pitched a no-hitter against Temple. The team was managed by first baseman Fred "Big Boy" Wills while Dred Cavender and future National League outfielder John "Chief" Wilson led the offensive attack.

15

In the early 20th century tobacco companies often included cards featuring images of baseball players in cigarette packs. Fort Worth players were the subjects of some of those cards, including Ike Pendleton, Charles Belew and Walter Morris (all seen above). Pendleton played a total of ten years in the Texas League including the 1908 and 1909 seasons with the Panthers. He is considered one of the most well-known and best-liked players of this era in the Texas League. He played primarily at second base and was a member of Corsicana's championship team in 1902 and San Antonio's South Texas League Championship team in 1903. Belew was the catcher for the 1910 Fort Worth team and Morris played and managed from 1910 through the 1913 season while he owned the club.

This was the last team owned by William H. Ward, who in 1888 gave the Panthers life as their first owner. Ward would either own the club outright or be part owner through a stock association club for the first 16 years of the club's existence. Ward's brother John L. Ward also played a role with the club, serving as the Business Manager in 1897 and 1898. The 1909 Panthers finished sixth in the eight team race but completed the season with a winning record of 73 wins and 71 losses. The team featured several players who took their profession to the major leagues including William "Kid" Nance, who managed the Panthers from 1913 to 1915, Roy Mitchell (20 wins), Sanford Burke (226 strikeouts), and Hub Northen. Reeve McKay won 20 games and Ike Pendleton and Dred Cavender, who also managed this team, were part of the fleet-footed outfield.

Roy Mitchell, Bill Brady, Reeves McKay, and Sanford Burk are posing for this 1909 photograph at Haines Park. Roy Mitchell was the star of this group, moving up to the St. Louis Browns in 1910 and spending the next seven years pitching for the Browns, Cubs, and Cincinnati Reds. Mitchell won 20 games with the 1909 Panthers and had earlier won 20 with Temple in 1905. Bill Brady only pitched in two Texas League seasons, but Reeves McKay threw for six Texas League seasons, winning 20 games for the 1909 Panthers and compiling a league-leading 22 wins the next year with Fort Worth and Houston. A left-handed hurler, he won 47 games from 1909 through the 1911 season. Sanford Burk, also a lefthander, played two seasons with the Panthers before moving to the National League for four seasons with Brooklyn and St. Louis.

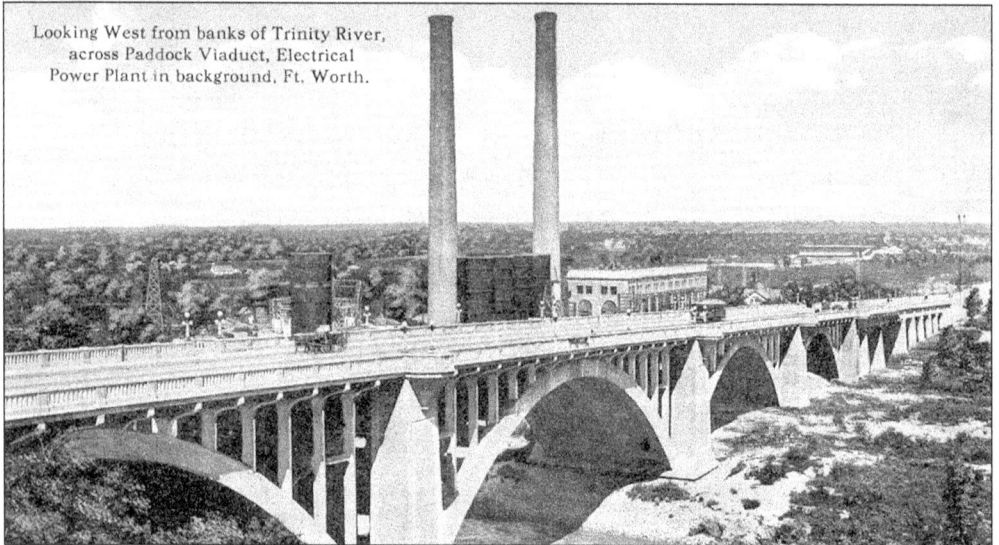

Looking West from banks of Trinity River, across Paddock Viaduct, Electrical Power Plant in background, Ft. Worth.

This 1912 postcard shows the view from the downtown bluffs overlooking the Trinity River to the north. The bridge was named the Paddock Viaduct and allowed traffic to pass north out of the downtown area onto North Main Street. In the upper right hand corner just below the horizon was the site of the first Panther Park built in 1911 and McGar Park that served as the home to Fort Worth's black baseball teams until being converted into a motor raceway. Further north on Main is city's stockyards that became home to the Swift & Armour Meatpacking plants. The cattle industry employed several thousand North Fort Worth residents whose homes were located in the area and whom would have easy access to their favorite baseball team.

18

During the early part of the new century Fort Worth Fire Chief W.E. (Bill) Bideker, (Chief from 1904 to 1919) was known to hire some of the city's ballplayers as fireman during the off-season. He would give them leave during the summer to play baseball and rehire them after the season. Jack Jarvis took advantage of this opportunity to work during his playing days and again after he retired from baseball. He became a Battalion Chief for engine companies No. 5 and No. 8. Frank "Swampy" Thompson, who played six seasons with the Panthers, also became a member of the Fort Worth Fire Department reaching the level of Captain for engine company No. 20 in 1931. This photo was made at Station No. 8 with Jarvis standing far right.

The electronic media and information available to today's fans were not available in 1915. Here the *Fort Worth Star-Telegram* newspaper erected a manual play-by-play scorebox outside their building so fans could keep up with out of town games. Fans would often gather by the hundreds to view the progress of the action. During the 1923 Dixie Series this display showed an away game with the New Orleans Pelicans and over two thousands fans shutdown Taylor Street.

TWO

The Amazing Twenties
1919–1929

On the walls of the Major League Baseball Hall of Fame in Cooperstown, NY are photos recognizing two minor league franchises for their outstanding achievements. The two teams are the Baltimore Orioles, who won the International League regular season seven straight seasons from 1919 to 1925, and the Fort Worth Panthers, who won the Texas League Championship six straight seasons from 1920 through 1925. The Panthers had also won the second half of the 1919 season but lost to Shreveport in the championship series.

This era in Panthers baseball is regarded as the greatest in their history. The credit unarguably rests with the ownership and management team of W.K. Stripling, Paul LaGrave, and fiery on-field manager Jake Atz. Atz would manage the team throughout the decade and maintain the longest tenure of any manager in the Texas League with one team. The decade would witness the birth of the Dixie Series and the building of a new ballpark that would eventually become LaGrave Field. A hero would retire to become an automobile dealer and county judge. The lead-off hitter for these great Panther teams would be a Cuban born immigrant and the dominating pitching duo of Joe Pate and Paul Wachtel would win a combined 280 games during the six championship years. The decade would end with the country facing a depression, the Panthers losing their long time manager, and the city losing one of its icons.

Prior to his front office positions with the Panther ball club, Paul LaGrave played three years with the San Antonio Bronchos and Galveston Sandcrabs teams in the South Texas League from 1903 through 1905. While with the San Antonio Bronchos LaGrave would become a teammate and friend of J. Walter Morris. This friendship and bond would help lead Paul to Fort Worth to work for Morris in 1911 and eventually take over the Panther front office in 1916. Prior to joining the Panthers, LaGrave wrapped up his playing career with Greenville (MS) in the Cotton States League, Helena in the Arkansas State League, and served as manager of Jonesboro in the Northeast Arkansas League.

Following the 1920 season, won by the Panthers in a runaway, Paul LaGrave and league President J. Walter Morris arranged a series with the Little Rock club, champions of the Southern Association. Though a championship series of some kind had been discussed in the papers for many years it is generally recognized that Paul LaGrave was the catalyst for making it come true. Known this first year as the Southern Championship, it became a fall classic between the two leagues and would forever after be called the Dixie Series. The Panthers success in the series was overwhelming, winning not only five of the first six contests, but continuing to win three of the final four they played through the 1930s and '40s.

HOFFMAN
2ᴺᴰ B

STOW
S.S

PATE
P

KRAFT
1ˢᵗ B

MOORE
C.

WILLIAMS
R.F.

HAWORTH
C

ROE

The Panthers won an impressive 108 games during their championship season of 1920. More impressive was that the win total outdistanced the second place Wichita Falls Spudders by 23 games in the total standings. This was the first team to represent Fort Worth and the Texas League in what would become the Dixie Series. The Little Rock Travelers from the Southern

APPLETON P   HALEY 3RD B.   WACHTEL P   O'BRIEN C.F.   PHELAN Utility   JOHNS P   SEARS L.F.   YELLOWHORSE P   WANO 1ST B.

Southern Championship
Ft Worth, Tex   VS

Association agreed to the series and were beaten four games to two with one tie. Joe Pate and Paul Wachtel began their heroics on the mound and Clarence Kraft, Ziggy Sears, Dutch Hoffman, Homer Haworth, Dugan Phelan, and Bobby Stow led the attack. Arlington native Ed Appleton and "Gus" Johns were also key members of the pitching staff.

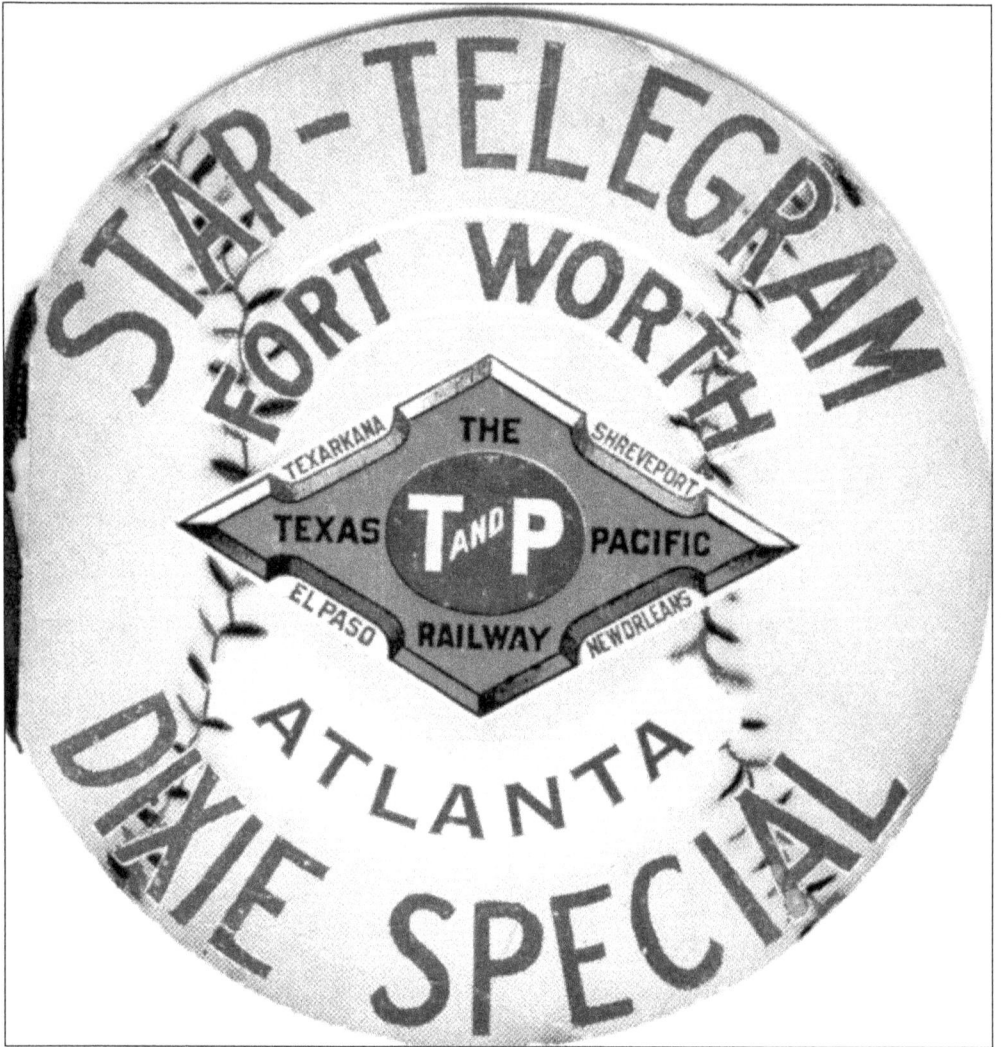

The Dixie Series was so special to Fort Worth fans a special train dubbed "the Dixie Special" was chartered by *Star-Telegram* newspaper owner Amon Carter to take patrons to the games held out of state. The first contest, in 1920, was not sanctioned by the Southern Association but a formal contract between the two leagues was written for 1921 and the series was played continuously through the 1958 season. There was an attempt at its rebirth in 1967 but it lasted just the one year. Over 36,000 fans paid admission to the first series and gate receipts totaled almost $50,000.

Clarence Kraft was the "Babe Ruth" of the Panther dynasty. Brought to Fort Worth by Paul LaGrave in 1918, Kraft played seven seasons with the Panthers and hit over .300 for five of them. In 1924 Clarence Kraft led all of baseball with 55 home runs, a Texas League record that would last for thirty-two years. On September 4th, with ten games remaining, "Big Boy" needed five home runs to tie the then major league record of 59 set by Babe Ruth. Amon Carter Sr. offered Kraft $10,000 if he were to break the record. Unfortunately, he hit only one more homerun and it came on the last day of the regular season. Kraft also hit for a .349 average and accumulated 196 runs batted in for the 1924 season. The 196 runs batted in are still a Texas League Record. "Big Boy" also had three at bats with the 1914 Boston Braves where he had one hit for a .333 major league average. Upon retiring from the Panthers the big first baseman settled in Fort Worth where he first purchased and operated a Ford dealership then later became a very popular county judge. His career slugging percentage of .544 also still leads the Texas League record books.

After the ownership change during the winter of 1916, Jake Atz became Paul LaGrave's first choice to be the full time leader of the Panthers. He had managed the Panthers for parts of three seasons from 1914 through 1916 but was fired in midseason of 1916. In all he managed 21 years in the Texas League and had a consecutive streak of thirteen seasons with the Panthers. Atz also spent three years in the American League as a player, his first with the Senators and his last two with Charles Comiskey's Chicago WhiteSox. Though never considered a consistent hitter he was forced out of playing when he was hit in the head by a Walter Johnson fastball. Born in Washington, D.C. in 1879 Atz eventually made New Orleans his home and died there in May of 1945.

Cuban-born Jacinto del Calvo was the leadoff hitter for much of the Panthers' reign as Texas League Champions in the 1920s. Calvo garnered 56 major league at bats in two seasons with the Washington Senators (1913 and 1920) and hit over .300 three times with the Panthers. He was recognized not only for his speed but his strong left-handed throwing arm as well. Calvo returned to Cuba every off-season where he played winter ball in the Havana League.

The first radio broadcast of a Texas League game happened in Fort Worth on Aug 30, 1922. The game info was relayed from Panther Park to the station downtown and broadcast over the airwaves from the station. The response was so overwhelming that on September 1st, WBAP sent Harold Hough to Panther Park to broadcast live from the field. The broadcast traveled a mile and a half from the field to the studios by telephone and was the first live broadcast in the south. Radio served to entertain thousands of baseball fans through the twenties and thirties and local broadcasts of their hometown teams were very popular. The Brooklyn Dodgers and St. Louis Cardinals broadcast extensively in the western states and thus many Panther fans also became Dodgers fans even before Fort Worth became a Brooklyn farm team in the late 1940s.

The Fort Worth Cats of 1923

The 1923 Fort Worth Panthers won 96 games and finished 13$\frac{1}{2}$ games ahead of second place San Antonio. Lil Stoner won 27 games and Joe Pate won 23 to lead the pitching staff while slugger Clarence Kraft (32 home runs and 131 RBIs) and lead-off hitter Jacinto Calvo (.342 batting average with 72 RBIs) led the hitters. The 1923 team faced the New Orleans Pelicans in the Dixie Series, winning four games to two.

For 11 years Joe Pate was the pitching mainstay for the Panthers. Pate was considered the staff ace during their incredible run of championships in the 1920s. He led the Texas League in innings pitched for four straight years (1922–1925) and is the only Texas League pitcher to have ever won 30 games twice (1921 and 1924). Overall Pate won 153 games during the Panthers' six-year championship run. He would move on to the American League's Philadelphia Athletics for the 1926 and '27 seasons; in 1926 he posted a 9-0 record with a 2.71 earned run average. Following his playing days, Pate spent nine years as a Texas League umpire.

The 1926 season was the first in six years the Panthers did not win the league championship. The Dallas Steers, behind Hap Morse and Snipe Conley, won the league by three games over San Antonio and six games over the Panthers. Elon "Chief" Hogsett (left), Jimmy Walkup, Dickie Kerr, and Paul Wachtel made up the Panthers' pitching staff that season as Joe Pate was now in the major leagues with the Philadelphia Athletics. "Big Ed" Konetchy, who had admirably replaced Clarence Kraft in 1925, could not duplicate his offensive threat in 1926. Hogsett went on to reach the big leagues in 1929 and in an 11-year major league career with the Detroit Tigers, St.Louis Browns, and Washington Senators he amassed 63 wins.

CHAMPIONS 1920 1921 1922 1923 1924 1925 CHAMPIONS

The Cats
1926

W.K. STRIPLING
PRESIDENT

Stripling's Department Store has been a fixture in Fort Worth for over 100 years and was started by brothers W.K. and W.C. Stripling. It was W.K. who came to the rescue of the city's baseball team. In 1916 Panthers owner Frank Weaver of Waxahachie, frustrated with manager's Jake Atz refusal to remove a pitcher, walked out to the mound and removed him himself. Atz left the team and was replace by Otto McIver. After the season Texas League President J. Walter Morris felt Fort Worth needed a more responsible ownership group and called upon W.K. Stripling and Paul LaGrave to buy the ball club interests. Stripling and LaGrave immediately rehired Jake Atz as skipper and thus began the success and dynasty that led to the Panthers of the 1920s. With the Panthers' success Stripling was thrust into visibility and prominence as a leader in Fort Worth. He was obviously proud of his team's accomplishments as depicted in his business card.

32

One of the most popular Panther players during the 1920s was shortstop Jack "PeeWee" Tavener. Tavener was brought in to replace Topper Rigney after the 1921 season when Rigney signed with the Detroit Tigers. Rigney had also been a popular player but Tavener stepped in and made everyone forget his Tiger counterpart. Tavener came to Fort Worth after only one year of organized ball but played well in the field and at the plate. He would follow Rigney to the Tigers after the 1924 season and played five years in the major leagues, the last with the Cleveland Indians. In 1927 Tavener hit .274 and stole 20 bases for the Tigers. He eventually returned to Fort Worth and played shortstop for the 1930, '33, and '34 Panthers. After his retirement from baseball Tavener opened "Tavener's Playdium," a bowling alley, on Camp Bowie Boulevard.

The combination of Joe Pate and Paul Wachtel was perhaps the greatest pitching tandem in minor league baseball history. Wachtel, seen here, still owns Texas League records for most wins (231), most complete games (242), most shutouts (32), most innings pitched (3177), and second with most strikeouts (1,359). His favorite pitch was a spitball that was outlawed in most leagues and but which was allowed in the Texas League. Thus, though capable of competing at a higher classification, he stayed in the league to use his famous pitch. In his six seasons with the Panthers (1920–1925) Wachtel won over 120 games.

FORT WORTH BALL CLUB, 1929

In January of 1929 Paul LaGrave lost a long struggle with illness and passed away. W.K. Stripling, upon learning of his good friend's death, decided he no longer wanted to be a part of Fort Worth's baseball fortunes. Shortly after the 1929 season began Stripling sold his and the LaGrave Estate interests to S.S. Lard and Ted Robinson. The team would later endure a managerial change in July that ended the long career of Jake Atz tenure as well. New manager Frank Snyder had spent 15 years in the major leagues but would only win two more games in the second half than Atz had in the first. The Panthers finished fourth in both half-seasons. Dick Whitworth, Dick McCabe, and Lil Stoner led the mounds corps while Lee Stebbins, Joe Bonowitz, Tony Rensa, and Les Mallon led the hitters. With the death of LaGrave Fort Worth baseball had lost one of its family members but he would forever be remembered when Stripling changed the name of Panther Park to LaGrave Field in his honor.

THREE

The Depression Era
1930–1942

The hard economic times of the 1930s had a major impact on minor league baseball clubs throughout the country. Attendance fell dramatically and many leagues folded, taking with them the franchises and cities that would never again see professional baseball. The Texas League maintained a strong commitment from the founding members but had to replace Wichita Falls and Shreveport/Tyler by expanding north into Oklahoma City and Tulsa in 1933. Shreveport's franchise had moved to Tyler in 1932 when their field was destroyed by fire but the club did not find economic success in its new home so the decision was made to include the Oklahoma cities.

Ownership of the Fort Worth club passed from S.S. Lard and Ted Robinson to Norman Perry, who also owned the Indianapolis Indians of the American Association. After only one year Perry sold out to a stock ownership group first headed by R.A. Westbrook and then Stanley Thompson. Thompson would maintain the club's President title from 1937 through the 1942 season when the league shut down for World War II. W.K. Stripling would also return as a member of the board of Directors in the late thirties.

The field managers of the era included Frank Snyder, Art "Dugan" Phelan, Dick McCabe, Walter Hoelke, a one year return by Jake Atz, John Heving, Harry McCurdy, Homer Peel, Jackie Reid, Bob Linton, and finally a 1942 stint by Hall of Fame member and Fort Worth native (for most of his youth) Rogers Hornsby. This managerial carrousel would be a far cry from the term of 13 consecutive years Jake Atz had at the helm of the Panthers in the late teens and '20s.

The Panthers were more frequently being referred to as the Cats and though the team never won the regular season league title they were able to qualify for the playoffs four times and win three Texas League Championships. In 1933 the Texas League instituted what was known as the "Shaughnessy Playoffs." In this format, which was becoming popular in minor leagues across the country, the fourth place team would play the first place team while the second and third place teams faced each other. The winners would meet for the championship. The Dixie Series was still in place and the Cats faced Memphis in 1930, Little Rock in 1937, and Nashville in 1939, winning all three. Only Rogers Hornsby's 1942 team failed to win the championship once they had reached the playoffs.

The decade started well for the Panthers when a second half first-place finish allowed Fort Worth to meet first half champion Wichita Falls in a best-of-three-games playoff. Fort Worth lost the first game but came back to win the next two and move on the face Memphis in the Dixie Series. The team was managed by Frank Snyder and was led on the field by first baseman Lee Stebbins and shortstop Jack Tavener. Pitchers Dick McCabe with a twenty-win season, Paul Gribble, and Dick Whitworth led the way on the mound. Fort Worth set the Texas League Opening Day attendance mark in 1930 when 16,018 fans herded through the gates.

An 11-year Texas Leaguer Lee Stebbins spent seven of those years with the Fort Worth Cats. He first joined Fort Worth in 1929, remained for the 1930 season, and then returned to play from 1936 through 1940 with the Cats. A member of each of the Cats three championship teams during the thirties, Stebbins was held in high regard by the fans. A left-handed hitter, he hit over .300 four times and was known for his habit of playing without wearing socks under his stirrups.

The 1930 season saw the first night game in Texas League history take place. On June 20th the Cats traveled to Katy Park in Waco, seen here, to take on the Navigators in the first regularly schedule night game. Fort Worth lost the game 13-0, but the attendance boost by playing games at night and allowing hard-working fans to attend games made the economics critical to continuing the league. Houston, San Antonio, and Shreveport would also add lights that first season while LaGrave Field would have their light standards raised for the 1931 season. Unfortunately, business conditions would force the Waco club to cease operations after the 1930 season. Though they started night baseball in the Texas League it would be as members of the Dixie (1933) and Big State (1947–1956) Leagues that Waco ball clubs would have to continue shining their light.

Dick Whitworth was the leader of the Panthers' mound corps for the first five years of the 1930s decade. The 1929 season was his first with the Panthers and he returned to the club every year through 1934. He then spent one year with Tulsa before returning to Fort Worth for parts of the 1937 and 1938 seasons. A great fielding pitcher, Whitworth won 20 games in 1930 and still holds the league record for total pitching appearance with 453 games, nine more than former Panther Paul Wachtel.

The starting catcher for the Panthers in 1935 was Waxahachie, Texas native Roy Easterwood, who would later to go on to play briefly for Chicago Cubs. The uniform Easterwood is wearing in this photo is actually Kelly green. The 1935 season was the only one in which the Panthers wore the green uniform, which was a response to the bright red uniforms Beaumont wore at that time. The green uniforms certainly didn't help the team's fortunes on the field as the Panthers finished last in the Texas League in 1935, winning 64 and losing 95. One notable member of that season's squad was longtime baseball scout and Fort Worth hometown hero Thomas "Tony" Robello, who is credited with signing Johnny Bench for the Cincinnati Reds. The Panthers were affiliated with the Reds for much of the thirties decade.

Pitching for the Cats in 1935 Lee "Lefty" Grissom led the Texas League with 166 strikeouts. He went on to spend six seasons with the Cincinnati Reds, and also spent time with the New York Yankees, Brooklyn Dodgers, and Philadelphia Phillies. In 1950 Grissom achieved notoriety off the baseball field when he faced manslaughter charges after a fight in California. He was later exonerated of all charges.

Zack Hurt became the first regularly scheduled announcer for the Wichita Falls Spudders' baseball team in 1928. He moved to Fort Worth in 1934 and became the Cats' voice on KFJZ radio continuously through the 1946 season. After years with his own radio show on the Texas State Network, Hurt moved on to a radio show in New York and replaced Bing Crosby on the new interview show "ABC's of Music." In 1946 Cats' games began to be broadcast on station KXOL and Bill Hightower was the voice of the team. KCUL and Lee Casper took over in 1951 before KXOL regained the broadcasting rights in 1955 with Augie Navarro, and then Cleve Griffin, behind the mike.

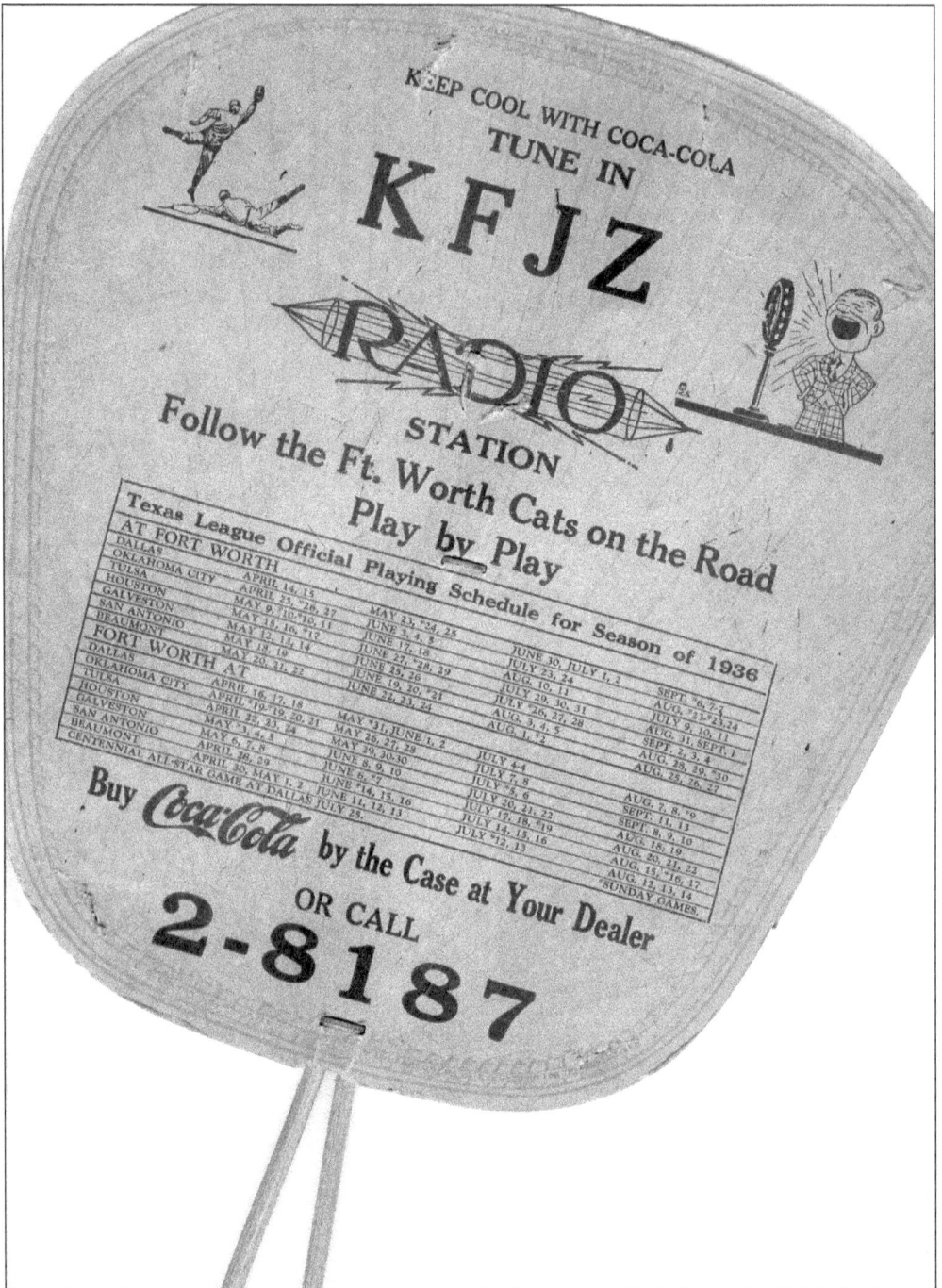

Radio continued to play a role in the expansion of minor league baseball during the 1930s. Television was still years away and the radio was the main entertainment device in many households. The Fort Worth Ball Club believed in the far reach of radio and led the way in broadcasting games. This fan includes the schedule for the 1936 season and an ad for station KFJZ, the long time broadcaster of Cats games. The photo also demonstrates that advertising gimmicks are not a new phenomenon in minor league baseball.

FORT WORTH BALL CLUB INC.

LaGRAVE 1936 FIELD

OFFICIAL SCORE BOOK

Coca-Cola

CALL A BOY

AND REFRESH

YOURSELF

The 1936 edition of the Cats improved to fifth in the league but were three games from reaching the playoffs. For the first time the season opened on a Sunday, two days before the rest of the league, so it would not conflict with a grand horseracing event at Arlington Downs. The Texas League All-Star game was inaugurated in 1936 with the event being played in Dallas. Charles Engle was the outstanding shortstop for the Cats and he set a league record for assists and total chances in a game on May 10th.

Charles "Red" English, not to be confused with Charles Engle, was the hard hitting second baseman for the 1936 Cats and he moved on to the major leagues the following season. English hit over .300 three times in his five-year Texas League career and finished with a lifetime .299 batting average in the league. He started with Galveston during the 1933 season before moving to Fort Worth and eventually playing for the Chicago White Sox, New York Yankees, and Cincinnati Reds.

A pitcher with the Cats from 1936 through 1942, Ed "Big Tracks" Greer, was the Cats' ace for much of his Fort Worth career. He won 22 games for Houston in 1933 and repeated the win total for Fort Worth in 1939. He won a total of 120 games over his Texas League career after having spent his first 11 seasons as a professional in the Western League. Though he never played in a major league game Greer was highly successful against major league talent in several of the exhibition games played against the big leaguers.

YOU WIN!

5¢

IF YOUR SCORE CARD CONTAINS ONE
OF THE LUCKY NUMBERS

See Inside Lucky Number Pages for Details

OFFICIAL

YANKS POUND REID,
SUBDUE CATS, 6 TO 3

5,000 See Greer
Out-Hurl Murphy
In First 5 Innings

BY FLEM HALL.

THE BOX SCORE

FORT WORTH BALL CLUB, Inc.

STANLEY A. THOMPSON
President

W. K. STRIPLING
Vice-President

JOHN L. REEVES
Sec'y.-Treas.

T. J. BROWN
H. A. WESTBROOK

CECIL L. COOMBS
Business Manager

HOMER PEEL
Playing Manager

KAY KIMBELL
CHAS. A. LUPTON

AMON G. CARTER
J. C. MAXWELL

Be Comfortable . . RENT A SOFT, CLEAN CUSHIO

In April of 1937 Lou Gehrig, rookie Joe DiMaggio, and the New York Yankees came to Fort Worth to face "Bear Tracks" and the Cats in a spring exhibition. Five thousand fans watched as Ed Greer pitched a masterful five innings and left with the Cats leading 2-1. The Yankees then jumped on reliever Jackie Reid and scored three in the sixth and one each in the eighth and ninth for a 6-3 win. Gehrig went three-for-four and DiMaggio one-for-one. The Cats' Lee Stebbins had four hits in five at bats while Rabbit McDowell had three hits in five at bats. This photo shows the program and newspaper story from the game.

Homer Peel competed for 14 seasons in the Texas League. Three of those—1936, 1937, and 1938—were spent as the player-manager for the Cats. In 1937 Peel led the team to another Texas League championship and led the league in doubles, runs batted in, and batting average (.370). His lifetime Texas League average was .325 in 1,430 games. Before coming to Fort Worth Peel spent time in the National League with St. Louis, Philadelphia, and the New York Giants before returning to the Texas League. He later managed in the Big State League before retiring to Shreveport.

Clyde McDowell served the Cats as a second baseman for six years, from 1937 through the 1942 season. He was named to the Texas League All-Star team five of those six seasons and led the league in fielding percentage in both 1940 and 1941. McDowell would move on to manage for Fayetteville, N.C. in the Cubs' organization and then become a roving instructor for the Cubs following that stint. Nicknamed "Rabbit," he wasn't a feared hitter but hit well enough to help lead the 1939 Cats to the Texas League championship.

Cecil Coombs played three years with the Panthers from 1921 through 1923 and hit over .300 for two of those three seasons. He spent a combined seven years in the Texas League as a player and later served as the Cats' Business Manager in 1937 and 1938. He was forced to take the field as a manager for three games during the 1938 season and is seen here preparing for a game. The 1938 Cats lost 99 games and finished last in the Texas League standings.

Shortstop for Fort Worth's championship team in 1939 and again in 1940, "Buster" Chatham played twenty-three years of professional baseball including parts of 1930 and 1931 with the Boston Braves. Standing only 5 feet, 5 inches tall Chatham was known as the "Little Giant" and he batted over .300 seven times during his long Texas League career. He later became a successful coach and manager and served the Waco Pirates as their general manager in the Big State League. Chatham was in the Waco front office in 1953 when a tornado struck the field and destroyed the ballpark. He told the story of a locomotive engine the railroad company kept close to the field offices despite the team's complaints of the engines location. "When the storm approached the business manager and I quickly jumped in the engine control room of that engine and it probably saved our lives. I never complained about that engine after that."

45

Stebbins Stoneham Chatham McDowell Kott Moon Cazen Suydam "Lala"
Keener Linton Greer Corbett Starr Doggett Metha Marberry Yocke
Fort Worth Cats 1939

The 1939 Cats team finished the regular season in fourth place but beat pennant-winning Houston in the first round of the playoffs and then disposed of San Antonio for the league championship. The Cats capped off their season with a four-games-to-three victory over Nashville in the Dixie Series. The team was managed by Claude "Bob" Linton and included several former big leaguers, among them Johnny Stoneham, "Buster" Chatham, Fred Marberry, and Ray Starr. Ed Greer was the pitching hero, winning 22 games and leading the league with a 2.21 ERA. Other members of the Cats included Walter Cazen, Hubert Shelly, Frank Metha, Carl Kott, Jack Suydam, and Walter Butler.

46

In addition to being a talented infielder, the Cats' Joe Abreu, seen here, was a practicing amateur magician and had been since high school. Several times he appeared in clubs and civic organizations with his magic. Abreu spent the 1940 and '41 seasons with the Cats before going on to have a short stint with the Cincinnati Reds in 1942. The seasons Abreu spent in Fort Worth were not the most successful for the Cats. The 1940 team finished last in the standings after winning the title the previous year, the 1941 team could do no better than fifth place and attendance and revenue continued a downward spiral. On a more positive note, Fort Worth did play host to their first Texas League All-Star game on July 11th of 1940.

Pitcher Fred Marberry, who had a fourteen-year career with the Washington Senators and Detroit Tigers, is sometimes recognized as the first relief specialist in major league baseball. He began his Texas League career with Dallas in 1936 and '37, but moved a few miles west to join the Fort Worth Cats in 1938, where he would stay for four seasons. "Firpo," as he was known, won 47 games in the Texas League and had the league's best ERA in 1936. As a member of the Cats' 1939 championship team he won 13 games with a 3.07 ERA.

Johnny Stoneham was an outstanding right fielder for the Cats and spent seven years as a Texas League player. He was a member of the Cats from 1938 through 1940 and was a key member of the championship team in 1939 when he batted .281. Stoneham hit over .300 his first three years in the Texas League and eventually made Tulsa his home. Stoneham also hit over .400 for McCook in the Nebraska State league in 1929 and played ten games with the Chicago White Sox in 1933 where he had three hits in 25 at bats.

A native of Hawaii, Henry "Hank" Oana, pitched and played outfield for five years in the Texas League. Three of those years he was a member of the Cats (1940–1942). In 1942 Oana won 16 games with only five defeats. The other two seasons he spent with the hated Dallas Rebels where he won 24 games in 1946. Hank played professionally for 23 years, spending the 1934 season with the Philadelphia Athletics and parts of the war years (1943 and 1945) with the Detroit Tigers. Oana later became a manager with the Austin and Texarkana franchises of the Big State League before leaving baseball.

The efforts put forth by batboys are never properly recognized, yet every player will tell you the batboys do much more than retrieve bats and chase balls. Their contributions actually will make a season much easier for many players. Through the years Fort Worth batboys have included little Jimmy Lala, who spent ten years with the team beginning in the 1930s, and Jimmy Walton (above) in the '40s. Later batboys would include Bobby James, Harry Mullins, Everette Roberts, Burch Coats, Gene McEntire, Harry Price, Johnny Woodman, Billy Hunter, and Kenneth Dockins among several others. The recent group of batboys has included Chris Gentry, Matt Treadway, and Tyler "Tank" Ramsey and all continue to be fan favorites.

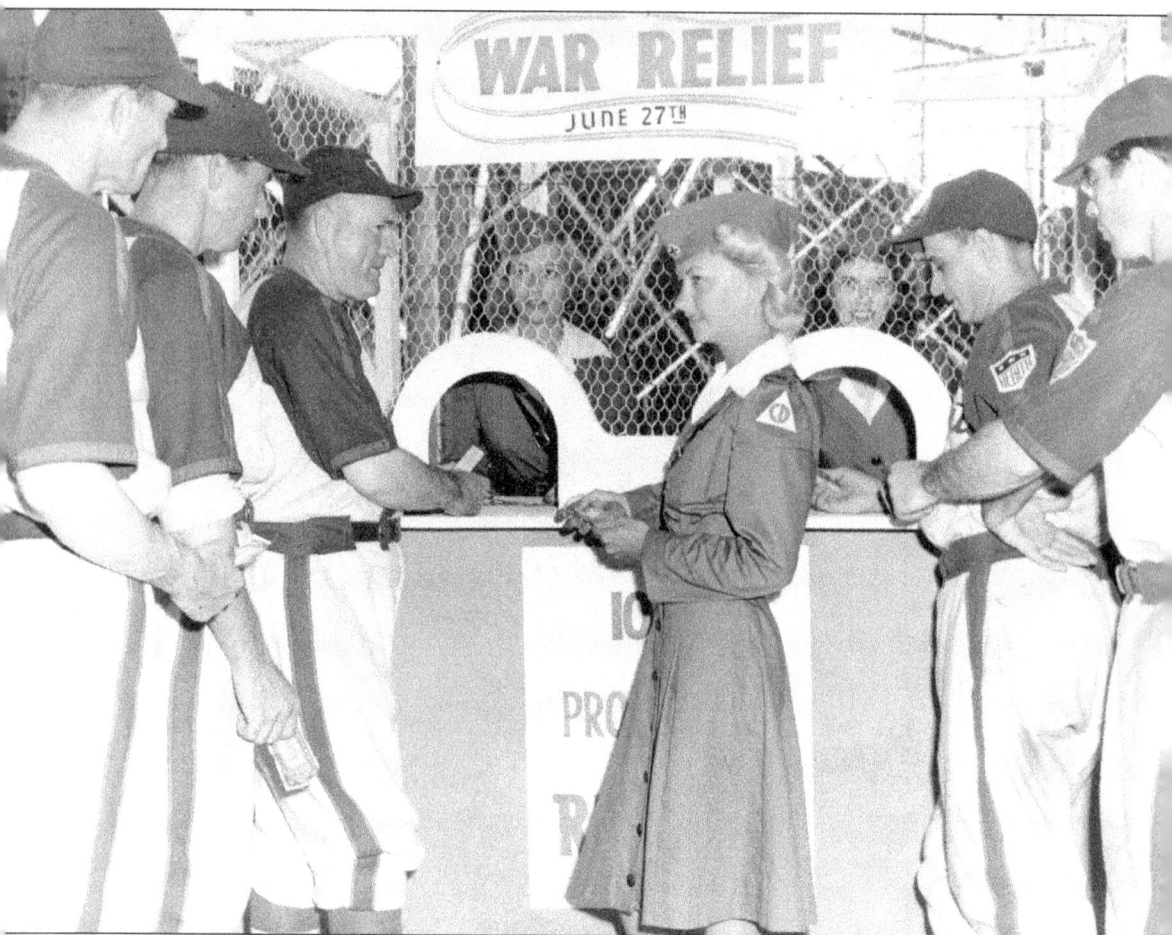

In 1942 Hall of Fame second baseman Rogers Hornsby, considered by many to be the greatest right-handed hitter in the history of baseball, returned to Fort Worth to take over the reins of the Cats. Hornsby and his family moved to Fort Worth in 1903 from Winter, Texas, when his family found work with the Swift/Armour Company. He lived and attended high school in the north Fort Worth area. Here, in this 1942 photo, Hornsby (third from left) and several of his players are participating in a War Bond promotion. The Cats had failed to make the playoffs in 1941 but under Hornsby's guidance they improved to finish third before losing to Shreveport in the first round of playoffs.

FOUR

The Dodgers Come to Town

1946–1956

This period in Fort Worth's baseball history is the most highly recognized era of the Cats as Instamatic and 8mm cameras began capturing photos and action movies of the players and games. Television also began broadcasting games, giving even further in-depth coverage to the events. There are many fans and players around that can still share their memories of those hot summers at LaGrave Field.

The Brooklyn Dodgers organization purchased ownership of the club after World War II and sent to Fort Worth some of the best talent available in Branch Rickey's farm system. The first year, 1946, the Cats' roster included Hall of Fame centerfielder Duke Snider and he was soon followed by Dodger greats Carl Erskine, Cal Abrams, Karl Spooner, Dick Williams, Maury Wills, and many more. Chico Carrasquel, Irv Noren, Don Hoak, Don Demeter, and others who wore the "Cats" emblazoned on their uniforms went on to have distinguished major league careers with teams other than the Dodgers.

The Cats won their last Texas League title in 1948 but almost repeated in 1949. LaGrave Field was totally destroyed by fire but rebuilt as a more modern facility for the 1950 season. The Cats tried a red pinstripe uniform for part of the 1950 season and short pants in spring exhibitions. Luckily, the shorts never made it to the regular season as one player commented, "I would hate to have the mosquitoes in Beaumont see these." The first televised game in the southwest occurred at LaGrave Field when WBAP TV televised an exhibition game between the Dodgers and Cats. It was followed a few days later by the first broadcast of a Texas League game, which featured Fort Worth and Tulsa.

The Fort Worth franchise entered the decade as a Dodger farm team but exited as a member of the Chicago Cubs system. Bobby Bragan managed for five consecutive years but the franchise would then see six managers in seven years. The Texas League (in 1952) and the Fort Worth team (in 1955) would become integrated organizations, but still have to deal with segregated travel to Shreveport. The decade would end with a major downturn in minor league baseball attendance but with a strong push to bring a major league baseball team to the area.

Branch Rickey's impact on baseball in Fort Worth cannot be measured. In the 1920s he was the architect of the farm system for minor league baseball and was a good friend of Rogers Hornsby, who had strong ties to Fort Worth. Rickey was general manager of the Brooklyn Dodgers when John Reeves negotiated the sale of the Cats to the Dodgers and was very instrumental in choosing to rebuild LaGrave Field after the fire. He was also very generous when it came to sending talent to Fort Worth and his later attempt to form the Continental League in the early sixties was a catalyst for the merger of the Dallas and Fort Worth franchises. Rickey made several visits to Fort Worth and had a great relationship with Bobby Bragan,who relates the story of a telegram exchange between the two: "Branch had already sent a letter to everyone detailing how we needed to save money by using fewer words in telegrams and the like. I received a telegram from Rickey asking if a particular player was ready to move up and I replied 'yes.' He replied, 'yes, what?'—not remembering exactly what he had written to me—but I replied, "Yes, Sir.' "

In 1946 the first Fort Worth team to take the field after the war raced to 101 wins and the Texas League regular season title. Fort Worth won the first round playoff series with Tulsa before losing to Dallas in the Texas League Championship series. The team's centerfielder that season was future Hall of Fame member Duke Snider, seen here, who batted for a .250 average in 68 games. Pitcher John Van Cuyk led the Texas League in strikeouts (207) and ERA (1.42) while Boris Woyt led the league in stolen bases with fifty. Fort Worth set a then club record of 273,659 fans in 1946, the first time they had reached the 200,000 mark in attendance since the twenties.

A reserve outfielder for the 1946 team, Maurice "Moe" Santomauro became the starting right fielder for the 1947 season. He played in 112 games and carried a .257 batting average in 1947 but it was his defense and exceptional throwing arm by which he earned his reputation. In a game on June 18, 1947, "Moe" threw home and forced out the same runner three times. Beaumont's Babe Glunt tried to score three times from second on base hits only to be cut down at the plate. After leaving the Cats, Santomauro continued playing in the Texas League with Shreveport (1949), Dallas (1950), and then made a move to the Big State League with Texarkana and Tyler. He and wife Katie made their permanent home in Cleburne, just south of Fort Worth.

14,845 See Cats Win, Tie, 1-0, 1-1

9/1/47

Noren Hits Homer in Second Game, Helps Save Opener With Throw From Outfield

BY LORIN McMULLEN.
Star-Telegram Sports Writer.

Before one of the greatest regular-season crowds in Texas League history—14,845—the Cats shaded the Dallas Rebels, 1-0, in the short first game, and battled to a 1-1 tie in the time limit second contest called at end of nine innings.

It was one of the best-pitched and best-played double bills of the year. It was ended to enable both clubs to catch trains for Oklahoma.

Between games Ferrell Anderson, chosen by rival managers as the Cats' most valuable player, was presented a sedan by Tom Abbott of Frontier Pontiac Company.

Abbott also handed Monty Basgall a $500 credit on a car and immediately fans collected an additional $1,300 for him.

Both Fort Worth moundsmen pitched three-hit games, Clarence Podbielan besting Joe Orrell in the opener for his 14th victory of the season and his fifth over Dallas, before Willard Ramsdell battled to a stand-off with the Rebels' Floyd Giebell.

Ramsdell deserved better. He was put in front in the first inning by Irving ... run into the right ... but a signal mix-up ... knuckle-ball ace a tie in the ...

Here, with Gene Markland on second as result of his single and an infield out, Short-

In all, the Cats rapped Giebell for five hits, including the homer and two doubles, but no two of them came in the same inning.

The double bill, which clo... the Cats' regular season pl... home for the year, put th... son paid attendance a... which for the second ... son set a new Fort...

The game ... intercity st... tories for ... nine fo... the C... of ... do...

... .ole ... n the open ... extraordinary greater support ... o rounds, when ... and Atwell came throu... brilliant plays.

TIGHT PITCHING

DALLAS.	ab.	r.	h.	o.	a.	FORT WORTH.	ab.	r.	h.	o.	a.
Markland,2	3	0	1	0	2	Pluss,cf	3	0	1	3	0
Smaza,cf	2	0	0	2	0	Basgall,2	3	1	1	3	2
Lipon,s	3	0	1	1	2	Noren,lf	3	0	1	1	1
Creel,rf	3	0	0	3	1	Anderson,c	2	0	0	5	0
Hirshon,lf	3	0	0	2	0	Atwell,rf	2	0	1	2	0
Moyer,1	2	0	0	8	1	Burge,1	2	0	0	6	0
Davis,3	3	0	0	0	0	Ozark,3	0	0	0	0	0
Finley,c	2	0	0	1	0	Brancato,s	2	0	1	0	4
Orrell,p	1	0	0	1	2	Schalk,3	1	0	0	1	0
Secory	1	0	1	0	0	Podbielan,p	2	0	0	0	0
2Borom	0	0	0	0	0						
Milstead,p	0	0	0	0	0						
Totals	23	0	3	18	8	Totals	20	1	4	21	7

Dallas .... 000 000 0—0 3 0
Fort Worth ...... 000 100 x—1 4 2
1Singled for Orrell in 6th. 2Ran for Secory in 6th. E—Noren, Schalk. RBI—Anderson. 2BH—Pluss, Basgall. SH—Schalk. DP—Noren, Anderson. LOB—Dallas 4, Fort Worth 2. BOB—Podbielan 1. SO—Podbielan 2, Orrell 1. R&H—Off Orrell 1&4 in 5. HBP—By Podbielan (Moyer). PB—Anderson. Loser—Orrell. —Capps, Fowler and Arceneaux. T—

SECOND GAME.

DALLAS.	ab.	r.	h.	o.	a.	FORT WORTH.	ab.	r.	h.	o.	a.
	1	1	3	1		Pluss,cf	4	0	1	2	0
	0	0	6	0		Basgall,2	3	0	1	5	4
	1	2				Noren,lf	4	1	1	2	1
	3	9				Anderson,c	4	0	1	6	3
	0	1				Teuple	0	0	0	0	0
						Atwell,rf	2	0	0	1	0
						Brancato,s	3	0	0	2	1
						...ark,1	3	0	0	9	0
						...urge	0	0	0	0	0
						Schalk,3	4	0	0	0	1
						Ramsdell,p	3	0	1	0	1
Totals	27	8				Totals	31	1	5	27	11

.... 000 001 000—1 3 0
.... 000 100 000—1 5 0
... Anderson in ninth. 2Burge ... or Ozark in ninth. RBI—Noren, ... 2BH—Ramsdell, Pluss, Anderson. ...oren. SH—Markland. DP—Lipon, ...land and Moyer. LOB—Dallas 3, ...t Worth 7. BOB—Ramsdell 2, Giebell ... SO—Ramsdell 6, Giebell 5. HBP—By Ramsdell (Finley). U—Fowler, Arceneaux, Capps. T—2:08. Att.—14,845.

another single in center and Smaza walked, filling the bases. Then Lipon lifted his fly to Noren.

Basgall speared Creel's line drive in the seventh, saving possible trouble there, especially since Schalk later committed a two-base error.

Aside from these two hits,

The rivalry with the Dallas ball club always led to big games and big attendance. This clipping from the Labor Day game in 1947 shows 14,845 fans piled into LaGrave Field to watch their beloved Cats win the first game and tie the second. During this period of minor league baseball curfews were in affect to allow both teams to catch the necessary transportation. Clarence Podbielan threw a three-hitter in the first game of the doubleheader with the offensive production coming from second baseman Monty Basgall. In the second game Cats pitcher Willard "Knucksie" Ramsdell dueled with Dallas' Floyd Giebell for the full nine innings and the score was tied at one apiece before both teams stopped to meet travel requirements.

54

(*above*) Williard "Knucksie" Ramsdell (right) was a mainstay of the Cats staff from 1946 through 1948. During that span he won 45 games for Fort Worth, including 21 in 1947. Ramsdell had a five-year major league career, spending two and half with the Dodgers, one and a half with the Cincinnati Reds, and one year with the Chicago Cubs. He managed a total of 24 wins and a 3.83 ERA in those five seasons. Ramsdell started the 1948 season in Brooklyn but returned during the Cats' playoff run to help Fort Worth take the Texas League pennant.

(*right*) A fireball throwing pitcher for the Cats in the 1947, '48, and '50 seasons, Bob Austin led the Texas League in shutouts in 1948. His earned run averages over that span were a miniscule 2.05, 2.75, and 2.90, respectively. An arm injury prevented Austin from reaching the majors but he was able to provide the Fort Worth fans plenty of excitement of his powerful right arm. Austin retired after the 1950 season and began a long career with an oil company in Panhandle, Texas. During one stretch of the 1947 season Austin either saved or won games in six straight relief appearances.

FORT WORTH CATS
1948

Top Row – GEORGE BROWN, GINO MARIONETTI, GEORGE SCHMEES, CHRIS VAN CUYK, GENE COSTELLO, GEORGE DOCKINS, DEE
2nd Row – DICK WILLIAMS, IRV NOREN, EDDIE CHANDLER, BOB BRAGAN Mgr., MERV DORENBERG, HOMER MATNEY, JOHN L
Front Row – JOHN PRIMM, Road Sec., WALLY FIALA, JACK LINDSEY, BOB AUSTIN, WILLIE RAMSDELL, DWAIN SLOAT, ALEX THOMAS, I
Bat Boys – BURCH COATS and EVERETT ROBERTS

Though many feel the 1949 team had better talent, it was the 1948 squad that brought the last Texas League title to Fort Worth. Ahead by 12 games entering the last two weeks of the season, the team lost the last ten games of the regular season but finished one and half games ahead of Tulsa. The Cats then dispensed of Shreveport in the first round and Tulsa in the championship round to win their last Texas League Cup. Bobby Bragan had taken over as manager in midseason and was awarded a trip to his hometown of Birmingham, Alabama for the Dixie Series. Irv Noren was voted league MVP in 1948 and Eddie Chandler, Carl Erskine, Dwain Sloat, and Willie Ramsdell played key roles on the mound. Dee Fondy led the league in hits and the team in batting average (.328).

A pitcher with the Cats from 1946 to 1949, George Dockins won 27 games during his Cats career and was the undefeated interim manager in 1948. Chosen to manage the Cats when Les Burge was released in June, Dockins guided the team to ten straight victories before Bobby Bragan took over the helm. This prompted Bragan to remark, "I considered staying away, not wanting to jinx the team." Dockins had spent the 1945 season with the St. Louis Cardinals, spinning a 3.21 ERA in 126 innings pitched, and he returned to the National League in 1947 for a short stay with the Brooklyn Dodgers.

Eddie Chandler was one of the many star pitchers to have taken the mound in Fort Worth. He would spend all or parts of four seasons with the Cats, ending in 1949. Chandler won 63 games as a Cats pitcher and got the call to Brooklyn in 1947, where he threw 29 innings for the Dodgers. He was traded to the Cubs organization and pitched for the Los Angeles Angels of the Pacific Coast League before embarking on a career as a financial consultant, eventually owning his own financial firm. Eddie, with wife Anne, made Las Vegas their home but he was able to make the trip to Fort Worth for LaGrave Field's opening day festivities in 2002. Chandler recounted an incident in Venezuela "I was playing winter ball and a local team asked me and another Cats pitcher, George Brown, to pitch for them. We refused and were escorted by bayonet to the local jail. The Dodgers and Yankees were in town for an exhibition and they arranged for our release or we might still be there."

Bobby Bragan Named Fort Worth Manager

BY FLEM HALL.

The Fort Worth Cats have a new, regular and—they hope—permanent field manager. He is Robert Randall Bragan, 30-year-old catcher who has been in the National League (except for two years of military service) since 1936. He is flying out of Brooklyn Tuesday and will take over the team in Tulsa Wednesday.

Bragan, who comes here with the emphatic approval of Burt Shotton, under whom he played in 1947, will take the reins from George Dockins who as acting manager since the discharge of Lester Burge, has won eight games, tied one and lost one.

The change is all right with Dockins. He didn't want the job as manager in the first place he said, and took charge between managers "to help out." He's well pleased, of course, over the 1.000 per cent ball the Cats played for him but will be happy to resume his old position as pitcher and coach.

"I know Bragan well from last year," says Dockins. "We spent a lot of time together in the Brooklyn bull pen. He's a fine fellow and I'll be glad to work with him any way I can."

Bragan, who lives in Birmingham, Ala., broke into professional baseball as an infielder in the Alabama-Florida League in 1937, played shortstop and third base with Pensacola, Fla., in the Southeastern League in 1938 and 1939. He went to the National League in 1940 when he started dividing time between infielding and catching.

Before the 1943 season opened he was traded to Brooklyn for cash and Pitcher Jack Kraus. In 1943 and '44 he served the Dodgers in his dual capacity in 74 and 84 games, respectively, batted .354 and .267.

He entered the Army April 19, 1945 and was discharged in time for the

BOBBY BRAGAN.

season in the bull pen working with pitchers. He has been doing mostly the same thing this season.

Bragan will be a playing manager for the Cats. He is rated still skillful enough for Class AA.

married (wife's name Frances) and has two children: Robert Jr., 6, and daughter Gwen, 4.

The move to bring Bragan to the Cats has been in the making since Ferrell (Andy) Anderson decided against taking the job. Four days were required to get waivers in the major leagues on Bragan.

Like Anderson, Bragan has had no experience as a manager, but, unlike Andy, Bob was eager to take the opportunity.

Bobby Bragan began his tenure as the Cats new manager on June 30, 1948. Sent to Fort Worth from Brooklyn, the Dodgers' replacement for Bragan on their roster was none other than future three-time MVP Roy Campanella. Bobby's tenure as the Fort Worth skipper lasted five years, during which time the Cats won 404 games and lost 297. They won the Texas League championship in 1948 and almost repeated the next year. In the seventh game of the 1949 championship series with Tulsa the Cats were unable to score Dick Williams from third after a lead-off triple in the ninth. Instead Tulsa won the game in extra innings, on a three-run home run by Joe Adcock. Bragan's greatest impact might have been his decision to make Fort Worth his home. His presence brought the Texas League offices to Fort Worth and he has had a great influence on the youth baseball leagues in Tarrant County. He was very instrumental in moving the Washington Senators to Arlington and also the rebirth of the Cats in 2001.

A young Bobby Bragan is peering over the dugout in this 1950 photograph. Bragan is still very active in the Fort Worth area raising funds to offer scholarship opportunities to local students with his Bobby Bragan Youth Foundation. Bragan's career has been well documented in his book *Can't Hit the Ball with the Bat on Your Shoulders* and other publications, but his impact on the people in Fort Worth cannot be measured. One gets a sense of his charisma and charm by hearing one of his banquet presentations or listening to him recite "Casey at the Bat." He was not only manager but also played in 487 games as a catcher for the Cats where he hit for a .270 average. To Bragan's right in this photo is Fort Worth Press sportswriter Blackie Sherrod. Perhaps the most popular sports columnist in Texas history, Sherrod had a long career with several newspapers before retiring in 2003.

Chris VanCuyk was a hard throwing left handed pitcher for the Cats 1948 championship squad. Chris and his older brother John, who also played for the Cats in 1946, both made it to big leagues. Chris spent parts of three seasons with the Brooklyn Dodgers, winning seven games and fanning 103 batters in 160 innings, while John also spent parts of three seasons with Dodgers. Chris's career with the Cats, which lasted from 1948 through the 1950 season, saw him win 14 games each season and strike out 367 batters.

Jack Lindsey played as a freshman at the University of Texas and was All-Southwest Conference before signing with Brooklyn. Primarily a shortstop, injuries and the arrival of Chico Carrasquel moved him to third base. Lindsey spent a total of four years with the Cats and in between seasons would attend SMU and TCU. He was another Cats' player who married a local gal when he married Velma Gauntt in 1952. Lindsey played the 1950 season with Montreal, the highest level of the Brooklyn farm system, and started 1951 with St. Paul before returning to the Cats. He would return again in 1954 for his last season in baseball and with the Cats. Lindsey continues a career in the insurance business and still calls Fort Worth his home.

ALL STAR
OFFICIAL SCOREBOOK
LA GRAVE FIELD

1948 ALL STAR CLASSIC

FORT WORTH CATS
vs
TEXAS LEAGUE ALL STARS

The 1948 Texas League All-Star game was played in Fort Worth before a league record 12,636 fans. This was the second year for a format in which the first place team at the half-season break would play a group of all-stars from the other league teams. The all-stars won a hard fought contest with the Cats, 4-2, when a tired Carl Erskine gave up two late runs while pitching in relief. The 12,000 in attendance still stands as a Texas League record for an All-Star game in the league. Only the two minor league All-Star contests (Mexico City in 1959 and Monterrey, Mexico in 1994) have exceeded that total. Fort Worth also hosted the classic in 1949, 1950, 1954, and 1958. From 1965 through 1968 Turnpike Stadium in Arlington hosted games where a group of Texas League All-Stars played the National League's Houston Astros. The new Fort Worth Cats will host the Central League All-Star contest in the summer of 2004.

Getting tickets for big games in Fort Worth often meant standing in line. Tickets were a hot commodity for games with archrival Dallas, Texas League All-Star contests and the many, many playoff games that took place in the city. When the Cats returned from Birmingham for Game Three of the Dixie Series in 1948, 11,553 patrons jammed into LaGrave Field to watch the Dixie Series action. The Cats lost that game on a seventh inning home run by Birmingham's Walt Dropo, but the excitement was not curbed and another ten thousand fans clamored through the turnstiles for the next day's Game Four.

60

The Dodgers sent rookie shortstop Chico Carrasquel to the Cats for the 1949 season. Fresh from Venezuela and not fluent in the English language, Chico had a tough adjustment to life in America. "All I ever ate was eggs and ham because that is all the English I knew," he once said. The ball club, wanting to make their shortstop more comfortable, hired Rudy Herrera as a batboy and interpreter. The fans embraced Chico and on July 25th celebrated a "Carrasquel Day" at LaGrave Field. "When they opened the centerfield gates I saw this car coming through the gate and thought they had given me a car," he recalled. "When the car got closer and I saw they had flown my wife and kids up from Venezuela, I started crying for joy." Carrasquel hit .315 for the 1949 Cats and proceeded to do the same the following season for the Chicago White Sox. He played six seasons with the White Sox before moving to Cleveland, Kansas City, and Baltimore for four more seasons.

BROOKLYN "DODGERS"

PITCHERS
11 Banta
13 Branca
16 Martin
19 Hatten
26 Barney
41 Taylor
12 Palica
17 Erskine
29 Podbielan
33 Ramsdell

CATCHERS
10 Edwards
34 Campanella
Narron

INFIELDERS
1 Reese
3 Cox
14 Hodges
42 Robinson
21 Jorgensen
36 Fondy
30 Hicks

OUTFIELDERS
4 Snider
6 Furillo
7 McCormick
22 Hermanski
32 Abrams
5 Brown

COACHES
27 Stock
31 Pitler

Burt Shotten, Manager

FORT WORTH "CATS"

CATCHERS
10 Bobby Bragan
23 John Murphy
5 Ken Staples

PITCHERS
14 Daniel Bennett
22 Carroll Beringer
12 George Dockins
21 Bob Houghton
7 Pete Giordano
17 Wayne Johnson
19 Joe Landrum
8 Mike Lemish
22 Bob Milliken
15 Chris Van Cuyk
19 Mike Nozinski
24 Mel Waters

INFIELDERS
20 Preston Ward (1st Base)
1 Wally Fiala
21 Al Leap
9 John LeGros
2 Gino Marionetti
18 Jack Lindsey
Bob Bundy

OUTFIELDERS
7 Walter Rogers
16 Sam DiBlasi
25 Walter Sessi
11 Bob Wakefield
3 Dick Williams
Homer Matney

WBAP introduced the first televised game in the Southwest on April 2, 1949 when they broadcast the exhibition game with the Brooklyn Dodgers. The Dodgers won the game by a 9-3 score with Jack Banta picking up the victory. Bob Milliken started for the Cats and had to face "Pee Wee" Reese, Duke Snider, Jackie Robinson and Cal Abrams in the potent Dodger lineup. Several days later on April 17, WBAP also televised the first Texas League game when the Cats took on the Tulsa Oilers.

Joe Landrum led the Texas League in ERA twice with a 2.25 and 1.94 earned run average in 1950 and 1952, respectively. Joe played four years with the Cats and two more with the Brooklyn Dodgers. Landrum's son Bill also became a very successful pitcher for the Cincinnati Reds, Chicago Cubs, and Pittsburgh Pirates. Landrum once wrote of his time in Fort Worth: "We traveled by private Pullman, had our own private dining car, and were driven by taxi to and from the trains and hotels. We signed meal tickets instead of the league standard five dollar per day meal money. I remember the old Cattleman's Café as a favorite stop with men in blue jeans and muddy boots jumping into their Cadillac convertibles without bothering to open the door." Landrum also pitched the Sunday afternoon game after the LaGrave fire in 1949. He also remembered the Vernon Woodman family who offered him and roommate Dick Williams a loft over the garage and a Model T Ford to get to and from the game.

Casino Beach on Lake Worth was a favorite hangout for families and ballplayers during their leisure time. Fort Worth second baseman Jack Lindsey remembers: "When I was single we would spend the day swimming at Burger's Lake, play the game that night, and afterward go to the Lake Worth Casino for dancing in their big ballroom. Wow, to have that energy today."

During the 1984 World Series two managers dueled to be the first manager in major league history to win a World Series title in each league. One was George "Sparky" Anderson of the Detroit Tigers, the other Dick Williams of the San Diego Padres. Both were former Fort Worth Cats' players. Williams played four seasons with the Cats and was on the 1955 Fort Worth team that could claim five future major league managers. He would hit over .300 in three of his four years with the Cats, leading the team with a .317 average in 1955. Here in this 1950 spring training photo Williams is modeling the team's new short pants, which were fortunately a short-lived experiment.

The Clover Grill was a favorite hangout for many players during the late 1940s and '50s. A lobster dinner could be had for $3.35 and a filet mignon with bordelaise sauce was only $1.65. The grill was located at the corner of 6th street and Main and just around the corner from the visiting team's Worth Hotel location. Bob Austin remembers the grill as a favorite among Cats players but not for Cats' manager Bobby Bragan. "Bobby would fine any player five dollars if he caught them drinking a beer but he would always tell us where he was going and he never went to the Clover Grill."

In 1949 John Reeves and Business Manager Robert Jones brought in 20 young women to begin the process of electing the very first Miss Fort Worth Cats. The final ten contestants were all given a small piece of luggage for participating in the festivities with the eventual winner chosen by the players. The final ten represented cities around the Fort Worth area and included Maurice Huggins, Juanita Simmons, Beverly Wren, Giny Lou Mason, Colleen Woods, Carolyn Shaw, Lois Gauldin, Jean Mussato, Vivian Livesy, and winner Barbara Fegin. Though she didn't win the 1949 contest, Jean Mussato returned in 1950 to win not only the contest but the heart of Cats player Dick Williams, eventually becoming his wife.

The very first Miss Fort Worth Cats mistakenly entered the contest underage and did not find out until later about the requirement. Photos were to be supplied with the application and Barbara Fegin didn't own a bathing suit for the pose. A Weatherford photographer entered Miss Fegin in the contest and mom came through with an appropriate suit. Cats' Pitcher of the Year Joe Landrum served as her escort the night she won the honor, which included a trip to Tulsa for the Miss Texas League competition. The Tulsa trip was great fun but Miss Fegin unfortunately lost to Catherine Granstaff, who would soon become Mrs. Bing Crosby. Miss Fegin married Herman Stroud and still lives in the Weatherford area with her husband and family.

Burgers Lake on the west side of Fort Worth still exists as a favorite swimming hole for many local families. During the heat of July and August days many of the Cat ballplayers would venture over to the spring-fed waters to spend their leisure time before a game. Here Bill McCahan, pitcher for the 1950 and '51 Cats, is prepared to get wet. McCahan won 19 games for the 1951 Cats, leading the team in wins. Before coming to Fort Worth he pitched four seasons with the Philadelphia Athletics, accumulating 16 wins and a 3.84 earned run average.

The starting shortstop for the 1950 Cats was Russell Howard Rose. Rose played 12 seasons of minor league baseball, primarily in the Dodgers organization, and spent 1950 and '53 in Fort Worth. He was one of the four players who held their wedding ceremony on a single night at LaGrave Field. Rose married Miss Patricia Ann Thayer from VanNuys, California with her friends and family in attendance. He also received his draft notice during the 1950 season but was able to finish out the team's schedule before reporting.

Marriages at home plate were not a new occurrence in minor league baseball, but as with everything else in Texas, it was done bigger and better in the state when the Fort Worth Cats had four players share their wedding vows in a single ceremony. Russ Rose, Joe Torpey, Johnny Rutherford, and Don Hoak all exchanged their vows on August 21, 1950. None of the four brides were from Texas but their families were all flown in for the event. The ceremony only took 35 minutes to complete and three of the four played in the ballgame that ensued. A reception for the players and fans was held under the bleachers following the game. The team was also wearing the red pinstripe uniforms they wore briefly in 1950.

One of four Cats to share his wedding vows at home plate was pitcher John Rutherford, who led the Texas League in 1950 with a 2.21 earned run average. His bride to be was Miss Martha Jo Day from Dayton, Tenn. Rutherford remembered much about his stay in Fort Worth and especially the wedding but said the fans of Fort Worth and the train transportation versus having to take a bus was a special treat. Rutherford spent the 1952 season pitching for the Brooklyn Dodgers and would return to the Cats in 1953, when he posted a 4.18 ERA in ten games. After retirement he became a very successful physician in Michigan.

On July 5, 1950, the Brooklyn Dodgers and Fort Worth Cats held a grand ceremony to recognize the opening of the new LaGrave Field. The day included a luncheon, a parade, the dedication ceremony and a game with the Dallas Eagles. Dodgers President Branch Rickey (seated far left) and Vice President Walter O'Malley (pictured at the podium) attended the ceremonies. O'Malley would eventually replace Rickey as Dodgers President and would soon replace the Cats as farm club.

Minor league ballplayers would often meet their future spouses at the ballpark or in the towns in which they plied their baseball trade. The fans in Fort Worth were close to the players and adopted many as their own. This included extending invitations for dinner and other festivities. Carroll Beringer tells the story of that first meeting with wife Jimmie, "Jimmie's dad had invited me and three other players over for a Sunday barbeque. I first met her when she answered the door. She had her pick of four ballplayers and I won. It was the best victory of my career." Carroll and Jimmie still make Fort Worth their home and can be seen at many of the current Cats' baseball games. Beringer also remembers winning the favorite Cat contest one year when fans and current friends Buddy Thomas and Joe Dulle stuffed the ballot box with his name.

Mike Lemish

Another of the Cats players to make Fort Worth his home was Gaylord "Mike" Lemish. Lemish played three years (1950, '54, and '55) with the Cats, winning a total of 28 games. His 14 wins and 3.33 ERA in 1954 were second to Karl Spooner on the team. Lemish started his Dodger minor league career with Moultrie, Georgia where he met his wife Christine and from where his minor league travels took him to Newport News, Greenville, Fort Worth, St. Paul, Mobile, Austin, and Dallas before retiring to south Fort Worth. Unfortunately Lemish passed away recently but he did see baseball return to Fort Worth and take part in the Cats' Opening Day festivities in 2001.

A great defensive outfielder, Gino Cimoli spent all or parts of ten seasons in the major leagues. His career began in Brooklyn with later stops in St.Louis, Pittsburgh, Milwaukee, Kansas City, Baltimore, and the California Angles. With the Cats in 1951 Cimoli batted .262 and led the league with 12 triples. He helped lead the 1951 Cats to and 84-77 record, which tied the team with the Beaumont Roughnecks. Unfortunately for Cimoli and his teammates, the Cats lost a one game playoff for the final playoff position and were the first Cats team of the new era not to make a playoff trip.

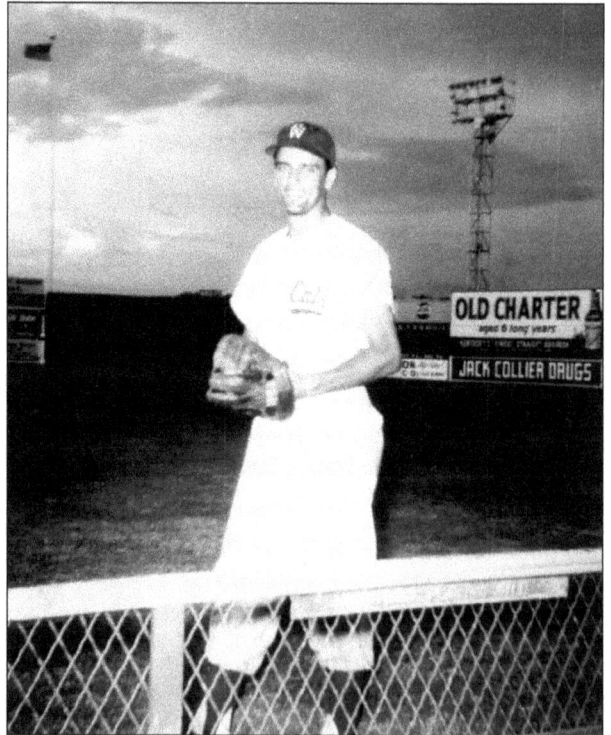

Opening Day was always special for baseball fans. The Cats' ownership and the city collaborated on several special events including an Opening Day parade. This photo shows Ted DelGuercio's ride westbound on Weatherford Street in front of the County Courthouse on April 14, 1952. DelGuercio played in 154 games for the 1952 Cats, batting .263 as their left fielder. He returned in 1953 for ten more games.

Joe Torpey takes his turn down the parade route in 1952 in this photo. Torpey, who had been one of the four Cats married on the field in 1950 (he and his wife Marilee still make their home in Colorado), had returned in 1952 for his third season as the Cats' second baseman. Torpey hit for a .267 average with six home runs in 1950 and stole 44 bases for the Cats in three seasons. The 1952 season turned out not to be a particularly successful one for the Cats as they finished six games behind the Dallas Eagles and lost to third place Shreveport in the first round of playoffs.

The first successor to Bobby Bragan's reign as manager of the Cats was Max Macon. Macon took over the Cats in 1953 and led them to an 82-72 record, good for third in the Texas League regular season race. Macon's playing career spanned five years in the National League, all before World War II, with St. Louis, Brooklyn, and the Boston Braves. After two years in the military, he appeared in only one more major league game in 1947. Macon accomplished an unusual feat by moving from the mound, where he had only seen marginal success, to becoming a first baseman and batting .273 for the 1944 Braves.

Elroy Face pitched for 15 years in the major leagues, primarily with the Pittsburgh Pirates. He had a career 3.48 earned run average and won 104 games. Face also saved 193 games in the majors, but for the Cats in 1952 he was a consistent starter, leading the team in starts (28) and finishing with 14 wins. His impressive Cats' earned run average of 2.83 was only fifth on the team amongst those pitchers who appeared in more than ten games, which says a lot about the Cats pitching staff.

Kenny Staples was the Cats' catcher for parts of four seasons (1949, '50, '53, and '54). He was another of the Cats players to find and marry a Fort Worth native and he recalls Cattleman's Steakhouse as a favorite hangout. Staples remembers the merchants were great to the players by giving them shoes, clothes, and dinners for good games and believes his favorite pastime was watching manager Bobby Bragan harass the umpires. In 1949 he hit .282 in 83 games as Bragan's backup catcher. Having fun and enjoying the game was always a part of baseball for Staples as this photo demonstrates.

Another of the very successful former Cats was first baseman Danny Ozark. Ozark averaged almost 20 home runs a season in the four years he spent with the Cats (1947, 1953–1955). He was one of the five members of the 1955 team to move to the major leagues as a manager. After several years managing in the Dodgers farm system Ozark was given the job of skippering the Philadelphia Phillies in 1973. Under Ozark the Phillies made it to the League Championship Series for three straight seasons, 1976 through 1978. As a player with the Cats in 1953 Ozark batted .300 with 23 home runs. In 1956, playing for Wichita Falls in the Big State League, Ozark hit for an impressive .350 average with 32 home runs and 101 runs batted in.

Karl Spooner was a hard throwing lefthander for the 1954 Cats and he led the Texas League in wins (21) that season. He also struck out 262 batters in 42 games before receiving a late call-up to Brooklyn. Spooner remained with the Dodgers the next season, winning eight games for the 1955 World Champions. Despite Spooner's outstanding season the 1954 Cats, managed by longtime Texas League icon Al Vincent, finished only fourth in the regular season standings. They did advance to the playoffs and beat regular season champ Shreveport in the first round before succumbing to the Houston Buffaloes in the championship series.

JOHN REEVES TAKES OVER
PRESIDENCY OF TEXAS LEAGUE

Fort Worth Club President John Reeves (right) finally stepped out of his Fort Worth role to become Texas League President in 1954. Reeves had been instrumental in negotiating the sale of the Cats to Brooklyn and was named president of the club in 1946. He later lobbied hard to convince the Dodgers to rebuild LaGrave Field after it was destroyed by fire in 1949. Reeves' tenure as league president lasted but one year before he turned the job over to Fort Worth resident Dick Butler. Spencer Harris was Reeves replacement as Cats president and he served through the 1957 season.

The 1955 team was the first integrated Cats team when Maury Wills and Eddie Moore joined the roster in July of that season. The team was managed by Tommy Holmes and would be recognized for having five members who would eventually became major league managers. George Anderson, Danny Ozark, Wills, Dick Williams, and Norm Sherry would reach the majors as managers. All of this managerial talent could not produce wins on the field, however, and the team fell to sixth place and missed the playoffs for only the second time since 1941. The team included future major league coaches Joe Pignatano and Carroll Beringer with Dick Gray, Mike Lemish, Jim Koranda, and Frank Marchio rounding out the starting lineup. Harry Schwegman, Frank Jeffers, Cal Felix, Rudy Paynich, Mel Waters, and Joe Landrum were also key contributors.

Tommy Holmes succeeded Al Vincent as manager for the 1955 season and it was his leadership that helped guide the Cats through racial integration. Holmes played eleven years in the major leagues, ten of which with the Boston Braves. He had a .302 career major league average and batted .352 for the 1945 Braves and even served as playing manager of that club in 1951 and 1952 before joining Brooklyn. Holmes had a minor league managerial career that took him to Toledo, Elmira, Fort Worth, Portland, and Montreal before embarking on a career as a scout.

73

Texas has a long unexplored history of hosting major league spring training during the early part of the century and into the 1920s. The New York Giants trained for 18 years in Marlin, the Tigers in Waxahachie, and the St. Louis Browns in San Antonio. In the early twenties the Cats would train in nearby Mineral Wells but also included other small towns around Fort Worth and Abilene. In 1948 the Dodgers restored an old army barracks in Vero Beach, Florida to become home to Spring Training activities for their major and minor league players. Vero Beach still serves the Dodgers today with a beautiful ballpark and several adjoining practice fields. In this photo from either 1956 or 1957 are Bill Saar, an unknown player, and Norm Sherry at one of the Vero Beach practice fields.

There are not enough words to describe Carroll Beringer's love for the game of baseball and dedication to the city of Fort Worth. He has spent tireless hours in fundraising events throughout the city including being the major force in re-establishing Texas Wesleyan University's baseball program and the Texas Ex-Pros Baseball Scholarship Foundation. Along with wife Jimmie, he can be seen at most of the current Cats games and still takes a hand in the festivities, handing out baseball cards to kids in a daily ritual at the game. Beringer pitched seven seasons with the Cats amassing 65 victories and posted a 1.63 earned run average in 1950. Beringer also won 19 games for the 1959 Victoria Rosebuds and was voted Pitcher of the Year in the Texas League. He later became the pitching coach for long time friend Danny Ozark at Philadelphia.

Mike Napoli was one of several catchers the Cats had during the 1956 and 1957 seasons and is probably the only catcher to ever lead the team in stolen bases (16). "I was a rare commodity; a catcher that could run," he said. "One year a speedster by the name of Bud Wilson came to spring training to race Jackie Robinson, when he asked who was the fastest in camp everyone said one of our catchers. He didn't believe them so we raced and I blew him away." Napoli has become one of the current Cats fans favorites and can be seen at most games handing out baseball cards to the kids with friend Carroll Beringer. In 1956 Napoli helped the Cats win 84 games and finished third in the standings. They faced the Dallas Eagles in the first round of the playoffs but lost four straight.

The Worth Hotel was the visiting team hotel for many years. Located on Seventh Street it was close to many of the downtown amenities and a short five-minute cab ride to the park. For several years some of the Cat players, who could afford it or not find a home immediately chose to stay in the hotel because of its easy access to the ballpark. Here, pitcher Joe Bielemeier and first baseman Ben Taylor are making themselves at home in one of the Worth's rooms in an early 1950s photos. Bielemeier spent parts of two seasons in a Cats uniform while Taylor, who had three brief stays in the major leagues, was with the club for one.

Fort Worth Press

FORT WORTH, TEXAS, THURSDAY, FEBRUARY 21, 1957

BROOKLYN SWAP
FW CAT FRANCHISE
APPROVAL AWAITE

VERO BEACH, Fla., Feb. 21 (UP)—The Brooklyn Dodgers and the Chicago Cubs today announced jointly a plan whereby the Dodgers would acquire Wrigley Field in Los Angeles for a possible transfer of the Brooklyn franchise.

— By BLACKIE SHERROD, Press Sports Editor

Dick Butler, president of the Texas Loop who attended the conference, said that he would initiate an immediate telegram poll of the directors on the proposed swap.

However, Leslie O'Connor, president of the PCL, has called a meeting for April 1 in San Francisco at which

time a vote will be taken on the transfer of the Los Angeles Club.

The LaGrave Field properties, approxi acres have been sold to a New York firm. T turn, have acquired a lease.

It was a complete reversal in parenth

It was a sad day in February of 1957 when the Fort Worth Press announced the Cats had been traded from their beloved Brooklyn Dodgers to the unknown Chicago Cubs. In Brooklyn there was more dismay as this move increased the chances of the Dodgers moving west. Brooklyn and Walter O'Malley traded the Cats to obtain the Los Angeles minor league team and more importantly the territory in Los Angeles. This they attempted to use as leverage with the borough of Brooklyn to build a new stadium for the team. As history recorded, 1957 was the last year the Dodgers played in Brooklyn but the 1956 season was the last in which they owned a part of Fort Worth. The 21.7 acres of LaGrave Field were sold to a New York firm and the Cubs leased the property. Spencer Harris was retained as the club president but for only one more season.

76

FIVE

The Demise
1957–1964

The pundits place blame on extensive television coverage of major league games and other entertainment for the great decline in minor league baseball attendance in the 1950s. A failure to properly market the game and provide exciting family entertainment should also be considered. Today's growth in minor league attendance is proof the minor league game can survive in today immediate information society. The games and leagues of today are a tribute to those that can market, sell, and provide an inviting place for families to spend their entertainment dollars. During the late fifties and throughout the sixties, however, the minor leagues struggled to survive.

In 1957 the Cats franchise was traded by the Dodgers to the Chicago Cubs for the territorial rights of the Los Angeles Angels. Brooklyn needed the territory in order to move west and as leverage with the borough of Brooklyn to build the club a new stadium. In Fort Worth the Cubs did not stir the same excitement the Dodgers once had. Though several future Cub greats would wear Cats' uniforms the passion had changed among the fans. Hall of Fame outfielder Billy Williams spent six days in a Cat uniform but joined the team on the road and never played in Fort Worth. To increase exposure and boost attendance the Cubs and Fort Worth management decided a move up a classification and thus played the 1959 season in the AAA American Association. This ended Fort Worth's long run as an original member of the Texas League.

The end for Fort Worth professional baseball would begin with the merger with Dallas. Several large markets including Houston wanted expansion by the major leagues to include their cities. When the major leagues refused they organized, with the help of Branch Rickey, a new circuit called the Continental League. It was assumed that Fort Worth and Dallas would be better served to join the new league as a joint effort and thus in 1960 the two organizations merged. The major leagues, feeling the pressure of the new league, finally surrendered and expanded but the Dallas/Fort Worth area was not awarded a team. The ownership group of J.W. Bateson and Amon Carter, Jr. decided to continue as a merged minor league entry and played in the Triple-A American Association (1960–1962) and Pacific Coast League (1963). The team was named the DFW Rangers and it would play a series in Dallas at Burnett Park and a lesser number of games in Fort Worth at LaGrave Field. By media accounts the team became more closely associated with Dallas, thus deterring Fort Worth fans.

When Tommy Mercer and Lamar Hunt took over ownership and operation of the club Mercer decided to resurrect the Cats as a separate entry for the 1964 Texas League season. Attendance and advertising revenues were not enough to keep the franchise economically feasible, however, and the last regularly scheduled game at LaGrave Field was ironically rained out. In 1965 the organizations and ownership again merged and became the DFW Spurs. The team played in the newly built Turnpike Stadium in Arlington and did return to the Texas League but it was a much different league at this time. This would be the end of professional baseball in Fort Worth and after several years of neglect LaGrave Field was torn down and sold for parts to communities throughout Texas.

The 1957 squad was the first to be affiliated with the Chicago Cubs but they also continued a working relationship with the Dodgers. The roster was filled with both Cub and Dodger hopefuls. Cubs' farmhands included Bob Will, Gene Fodge, Frank Ernaga, Joe Hannah, and former Negro League player Lorenzo "Piper" Davis while Carroll Beringer, Mike Napoli, Larry Sherry, and Frank Marchio represented the Dodgers. The club finished with 70 wins and a sixth place standing under manager and former Cubs scout Gene Handley. Murray Wall of Dallas threw a nine-inning no-hitter against the Cats but lost when the Cats scored a run in the 13th inning. The season would also be the last for Texas League stability. Struggling attendance in Shreveport (40,919) and Oklahoma City forced both franchises to move. Shreveport moved to Victoria, Texas and Oklahoma City moved to Corpus Christi for the 1958 season. This was only the second relocation of Texas League cities since 1938. The Beaumont Exporters had moved to Austin after the 1955 season.

A positive for Fort Worth came when Cubs ownership assigned slugger Joe Macko to the Cats. Macko has been a special part of Fort Worth's and Dallas' baseball history for over 50 years. He started his Texas League career with Tulsa and Dallas but spent two years with the Cats, 1958 and 1959. He led the 1958 Cats with 24 home runs and played 104 games with the 1959 Cats before being traded to the Minneapolis Millers. He returned to Fort Worth at the end of that season when the two teams met in American Association playoffs. The Millers beat the Cats in seven games and propelled themselves into a Little World Series match-up with Havana. Macko had nine home runs in the three rounds of playoffs to lead the Millers hitters. Macko turned to the front office after his playing career and became the general manager for the Dallas/Fort Worth Spurs. He soon began a long career as the Visiting Clubhouse Manager for the Texas Rangers and still spends many hours in support of youth baseball, baseball organizations, and the Steve Macko Scholarship Fund, which is named for his son.

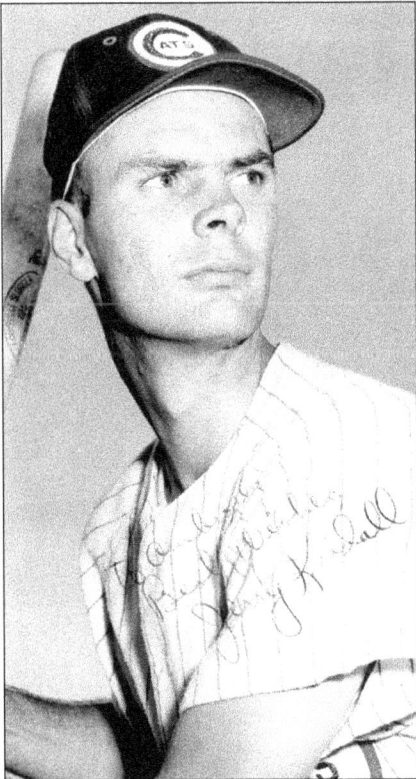

Jerry Kindall was a second baseman for the Chicago Cubs before being demoted to Fort Worth for the 1958 and 1959 seasons. He returned to the Cubs in 1960 and continued his major league career as a member of the Cleveland Indians and Minnesota Twins. Kindall was the Twins' second baseman for most of their American League pennant-winning season in 1965. He moved on to become an assistant coach at University of Minnesota before becoming the long time coach of the Arizona Wildcats in 1973. Kindall coached Arizona baseball teams to 861 victories and three NCAA titles in 24 seasons. He was Division I coach of the year three times and only recently retired.

Fort Worth's shortstop for the two years as a Cubs' franchise was Ray Bellino. Almost never missing a game he played in 151 games his first season and another 159 the second. Though he never made it to the big leagues Bellino was a fan favorite during his time in Fort Worth. The 1959 Cats were the first Cats team to play outside the Texas League. The triple-A American Association brought a new set of opponents to Fort Worth that included Indianapolis, Louisville, St. Paul, Minneapolis, as well as fellow former Texas League members Dallas and Houston. St. Paul had become a Dodgers farm team and many of the former Cats were now visiting as members of the Saints.

Named the Dallas-Fort Worth Rangers, the 1960 entry from the area was the first combined entry in the triple-A American Association. Former New York Yankee great Don Larsen attempted a comeback with the Rangers and Jim Fanning, who had played with the Cats a few years earlier, managed the club. The team was a Kansas City Athletics farm team but unfortunately finished last in the eight-team league. Former Houston Buffaloes and Austin Senators owner/president Allen Russell was hired in midseason as the General Manager for the team.

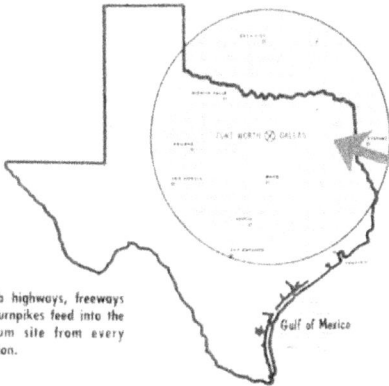

The population growth in Dallas and Fort Worth convinced city leaders they were ready for a major league franchise. The economic engine that a big league club would power was worth the effort. J. W. Bateson, a prominent general contractor, and Amon Carter, Jr., President of his dad's Carter Publications Corporation, teamed to bring an expansion team to the area. The original plans called for a domed stadium to be built in Arlington that would have been the first domed venue for a professional franchise. When the Continental League collapsed so did the dreams of major league baseball in Dallas and Fort Worth. Instead Houston was awarded a big league franchise and later built the Astrodome. It would take another twelve years and an extraordinary effort by Tom Vandergriff and others to finally bring the Washington Senators to town in 1972. The management team decided to remain organized as a combined minor league team and continue play as a member of the AAA American Association.

DALLAS-FT. WORTH BASEBALL ASSOCIATION

RANGERS

Price 15¢

1961
OFFICIAL SCOREBOOK

As evidence by this 1961 program cover Fort Worth and Dallas were—and still are—considered very different cultures. The majority of games were being played in Dallas at this time and the city of Fort Worth was losing interest in what was becoming more and more a Dallas entity. The American Association shrunk to six teams in 1961 and the Rangers finished fifth of the six teams. Indianapolis, Denver, Houston, Louisville, and Omaha all made visits to LaGrave and Burnett Fields. Managed by former big leaguer Walker Cooper, the team was now a Los Angeles Angels farm team, that new organization's first farm team (the relationship would last through 1962). Jim Fregosi was the shortstop; future big league manager Chuck Tanner roamed the outfield while Dean Chance and Dick Littlefield climbed the mound as two of the standout pitchers.

Brothers Joe and Jack Hannah, both former professional baseball players, are the founding members of the Sons of the San Joaquin, Western singing group whose sounds are said to be much like that of the original Sons of the Pioneers. The group has been featured at venues ranging from Carnegie Hall to Fort Worth's White Elephant Saloon. Joe played for the Cats as a catcher in 1957 and was in the Cubs organization for much of his career. His first daughter Jill was born in Fort Worth days after arriving in the city when transferred to the Cats from Memphis. Joe batted .244 in 52 games with Fort Worth and also played seasons with Toronto, Charleston, Hawaii, and San Jose. Jack, whose career was spent primarily in the Milwaukee Braves farm system, played for the 1961 and '62 DFW Rangers and had a 3.30 earned run average in 52 games with the '61 team.

Warner Western Recording Artists

SONS OF THE SAN JOAQUIN

FRIDAY, JANUARY 24, at 8:30 pm

From California's San Joaquin Valley, brothers Jack and Joe Hannah, along with Joe's son Lon, are remarkable vocalists. From a lifetime of family singing have come their airtight three-part cowboy harmonies which are in great demand internationally.

"The Sons of the San Joaquin are the only singing group alive who I feel sound like the original Sons of the Pioneers." -Roy Rogers

Bob Baillargeon became a recognized figure in Fort Worth and Dallas automobile circles as the former owner of Baillargeon Ford. Baillargeon pitched for the 1962 and '63 DFW Rangers and was a member of the last Cats team in 1964. He came within one out of a no-hitter for the '62 Rangers when facing the Indianapolis Indians. Despite Baillargeon's outstanding effort, the 1962 Rangers, which were managed by Dick Littlefield, returned to the bottom of the league standings. The American Association disbanded after that season, forcing the Rangers to move to the Pacific Coast League for the 1963 season.

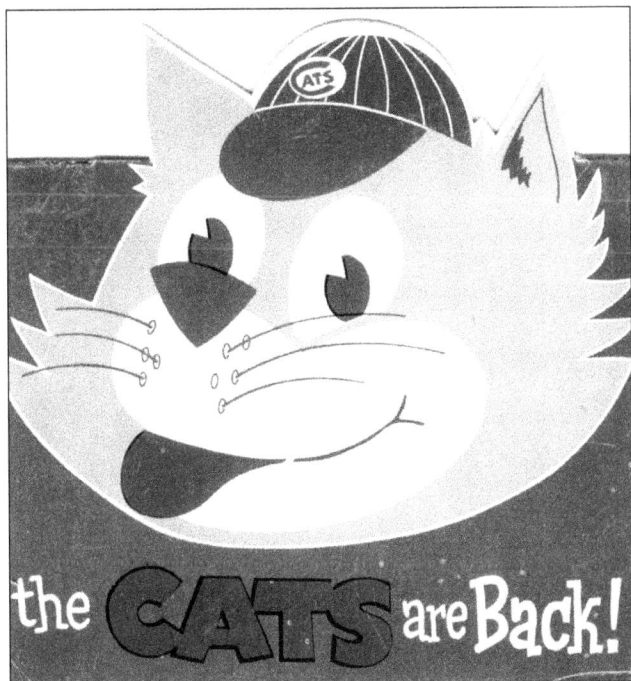

the CATS are Back!

The announcement of Fort Worth's return to the Texas League and their independence from Dallas was heralded as a rebirth for Fort Worth baseball. Tommy Mercer and Lamar Hunt, who together formed Mercer-Hunt Baseball, Inc., owned both the Fort Worth Cats and the Dallas Rangers in the Pacific Coast League. L.D. Lewis was rightly hired as the general manager for the Cats after putting many years into the organization's front office. Lewis started as an usher with the Cats in 1941 and eventually moved up to become business manager in charge of running the Fort Worth operations after the merger. He continued on as general manager of the Spurs through the 1966 season.

Alex Grammas was named manager of the new Fort Worth Cats in 1964 and future major league manager John Felske, pictured on the right, was the starting catcher. The pitching staff featured Dick Burwell, who led the Texas League in ERA with a 2.55 earned run average, and George Lance, pictured on the left, who had a 3.69 ERA in 33 outings. The Cats started the season well but lost ground on the first division and ended last in the standings. The team was second in the league in attendance at 93,574 but roughly one-third of that total was attributed to a few key dates when tickets were given away. (Tulsa led the league in attendance by drawing over 200,000 fans.) The last pitcher to take the mound for the Cats in 1964 also became the first to take the mound in 1965 as a member of the Dallas/Fort Worth Spurs. Bob Flynn pitched a complete game in a 1-0 loss to Tulsa in Tulsa on the final day of the 1964 Texas League campaign. He also came out on top in what would be the team's last win at LaGrave Field when he pitched a complete game seven-hitter, beating future Hall of Fame member Steve Carlton and the Tulsa Oilers by a 7-1 score on September 3rd. The last game played in Fort Worth was a Friday night loss to Tulsa. Another game at LaGrave was on the schedule for September 5th but was rained out.

This exhibition program from the 1964 preseason is a good reminder of the major league teams that have visited Fort Worth and LaGrave Field over the years. Jackie Robinson, Lou Gehrig, Warren Spahn, Hank Aaron, and Don Drysdale are but a few members of Baseball's Hall of Fame who made appearances at LaGrave during their playing careers. In this game on April 10th, former Cats players Bob Will, Billy Williams, and Dick Ellsworth of the Cubs took on Dick Williams of the Red Sox. Hall of Fame members Lou Brock, Ernie Banks, and Carl Yastrzemki are listed on the rosters.

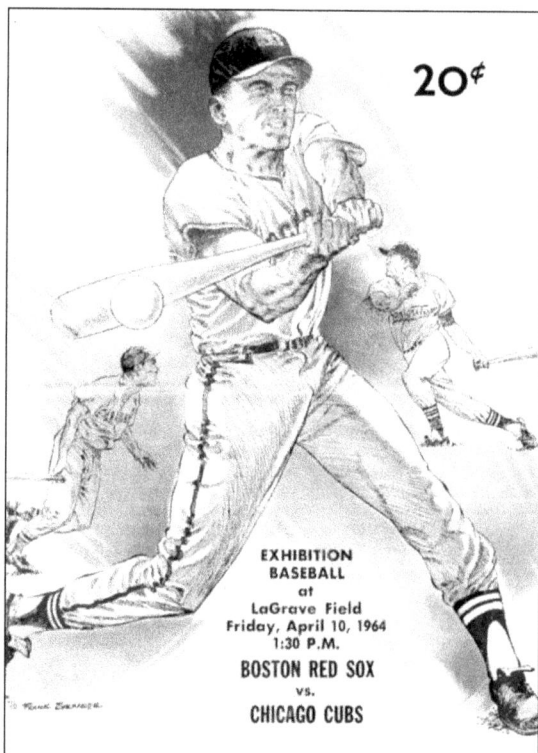

20¢

EXHIBITION
BASEBALL
at
LaGrave Field
Friday, April 10, 1964
1:30 P.M.

BOSTON RED SOX
vs.
CHICAGO CUBS

1971 DALLAS-FORT WORTH SPURS

Top Row: Terry Wilshusen, Mike Reinbach, Don Hood, Mike Herson, Carroll Moulden, Jesse Jefferson, Dyar Miller, Doug DeCinces, Enos Cabell.
Second Row: Trainer Ron Rouden, Steve Turigliatto, Tom Creola, Wayne Garland, Tom Walker, Steve Green, Randy Cohen, Gen. Mgr. Joe Macko.
First Row: Bat Boy Cory Phillips, Mark Weems, Javier Andino, Paul Flumer, Manager Cal Ripken, Leon Brown, Junior Kennedy, Pete Watts, Bat Boy Brent Kinman.

From 1965 through the 1971 season the only minor league baseball in the area was played a few miles east of Fort Worth in the city Arlington at the new Turnpike Stadium. Attendance would soar in the new confines with the team securing the highest attendance total of any minor league team in 1965. The Dallas-Fort Worth Spurs would become members of the Chicago Cubs and Houston Astros farm systems before moving their affiliation to the World Champion Baltimore Orioles system. The last minor league team to represent the two cities was this 1971 Dallas-Fort Worth Spurs team managed by Cal Ripken, Sr. (with little Cal Ripken, Jr. working the summer as a bat and ball boy for his father). Future big leaguers Enos Cabell, Bobby Grich, and current Chicago Cubs manager Don Baylor were all part of Spurs teams.

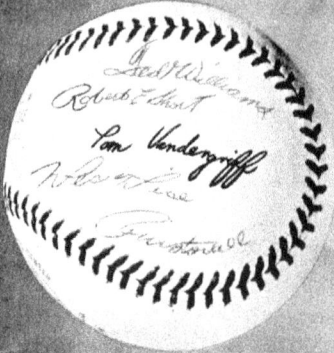

As fate would have it, when the Continental League forced the major leagues to expand in 1960 one of the expansion teams created was the 1961 Washington Senators. This happened after the American League approved the move of the original Washington Senators to Minneapolis to become the Twins. It was this Senators expansion team that Arlington mayor Tom Vandergriff and the leadership of Dallas and Fort Worth fought to bring to the area and become their first major league team. The Texas Rangers were born in 1972 with Hall of Fame hitter Ted Williams as their manager and little-known Wayne Terwilliger as their third base coach. The Rangers' history has been chronicled in many books but Wayne Terwilliger is continuing to write new chapters as a new member of the Texas Baseball Hall of Fame and the current manager of the new Fort Worth Cats. Readers will find photos from the Rangers' 30-plus year history in our other work, "Professional Baseball in Dallas."

Six

The Ballparks of Fort Worth

The city of Fort Worth was making the transition from outpost to urban center during the late 1870s but hard economic times were hindering expansion of the city. The town desperately needed business growth and citizens were frustrated with the struggle of the railroad to reach their city from the east. Gathering volunteers from all over Tarrant County the town took matters into its own hands to clear land and lay tracks to the southern boundary of the town square. The new railroad line was owned and operated by the Texas & Pacific Railroad and Fort Worth donated a large parcel of the town's southern area to become the T&P passenger and switching station. This area became a transportation hub for the city and would also become home to the city's first professional baseball team.

The original Panthers played in four locations around downtown, beginning with the first grandstand built in 1888 on the T&P grounds. That field lasted but two years before being torn down in the name of progress. The Texas League and Fort Worth fielded teams a scattering of six of the next ten years and thus the club did not build a permanent facility, choosing instead to play on the grounds of the Spring Palace which had replaced the original site. In 1902 Haines Park, which was located southeast of downtown at the southeast corner of Pacific and Pine, became the second facility built by the ball club. It served as the home field until 1911 when J. Walter Morris and the Panthers moved north of downtown and across the Trinity River into their new Panther Park. Unfortunately the levy around the north side of the river was not fully developed and flooding became a problem as the park suffered major damage in 1916 and 1920. The final move was in 1926 to a new Panther Park, which would eventually become known as LaGrave Field, on the east side of North Main. This location became the long time home to Fort Worth professional baseball and the historic site serves today as the home of the current Fort Worth Cats.

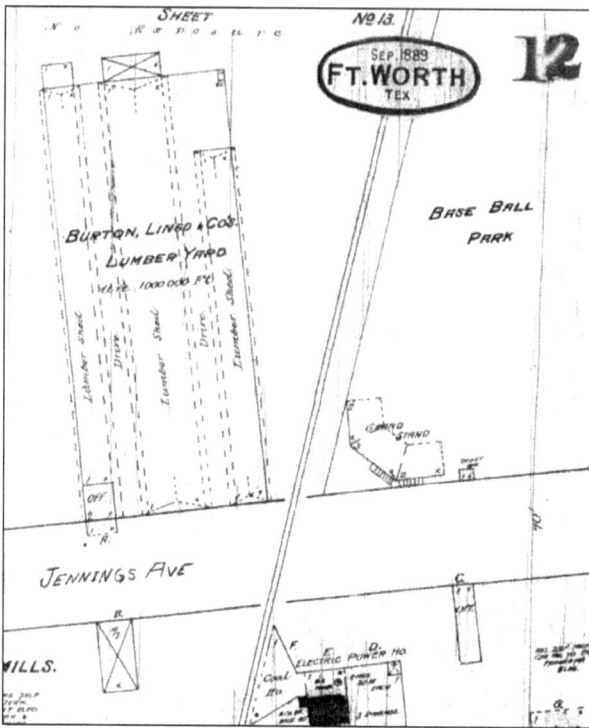

The T&P Reservation was an area of railroad yards located south of what was then North Street or Front Street (now Lancaster) and north of South or Railroad Street (now Vickery Blvd). Built for the 1888 season the ballpark had a small wooden grandstand that held approximately 1,200 fans. This Sanborn map of 1889 shows the grandstand just east of Jennings Avenue, with the railroad tracks running along the third base line. This park would serve as the home to the Panthers for two years.

In 1889 the city fathers felt the city needed an exhibition hall to showcase to the world the agricultural wonders of the North Texas area. The city built the Texas Spring Palace in the area of the T&P Reservation just east of the original ballpark. The Palace was a two story wooden structure built for hosting and promoting the county's and city's farming, ranching, and industrial accomplishments. The first Exposition held at the facility had a four-week run from May 29th through June 20th and was so successful the city would again hold the Exposition the following year. The original ballpark was torn down to build the Palace but an area of the Palace grounds were later used for the playing field. When the Spring Palace was destroyed by fire in 1890 the site again became an empty area known as the T&P Reservation. Since the Panthers played sparingly over the next ten years only a semi-permanent ball field known as the Texas and Pacific Park was built for home games.

The resurrection of the Texas League in 1902 caused a great excitement on the part of city leaders in Fort Worth. The resources were gathered and a new ballpark was constructed on the southeast corner of Pine and Pacific (now E. Predidio St.). Haines Park had a seating capacity of 1,500 and would be the first Fort Worth field to include an outfield fence with advertising signage. The contractor was Mr. Churchill who built a roof over the stands and installed a nine-foot fence surrounding the outfield. The first practice was held at the park on April 17th and the first exhibition game was played on April 22nd. In the official league home opener the Panthers hosted the Dallas Hams and lost twelve to nine when the Panthers allowed a seven run eighth inning. The site is currently home to Fort Worth's Transportation Company depot.

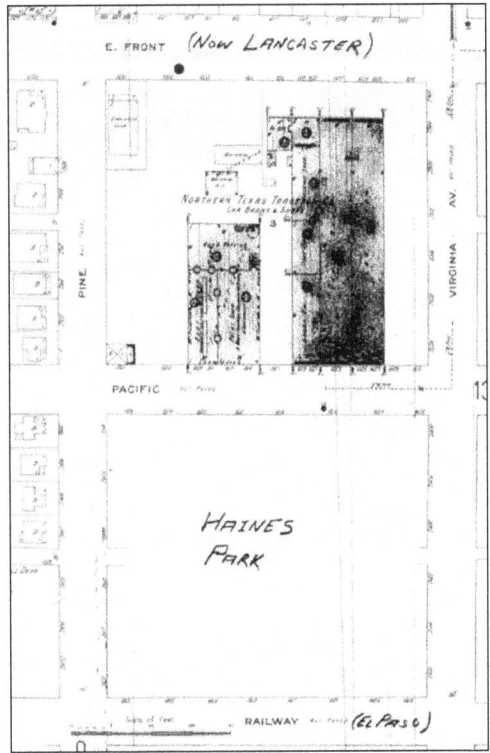

Haines Park was expanded in 1904 when the team added 60 feet of bleachers and extended the existing grandstand by 100 feet. J. Walter Morris and associates bought the ball club during the winter of 1909 and immediately added 1,000 seats and dressing rooms for both the home and visiting teams. They also announced before the 1910 season opener that they had purchased five acres on the north side of downtown, below the bluffs, to build a new ballpark for the 1911 season. This photo shows the few downtown buildings tall enough to be seen over the outfield fence of Haines Park.

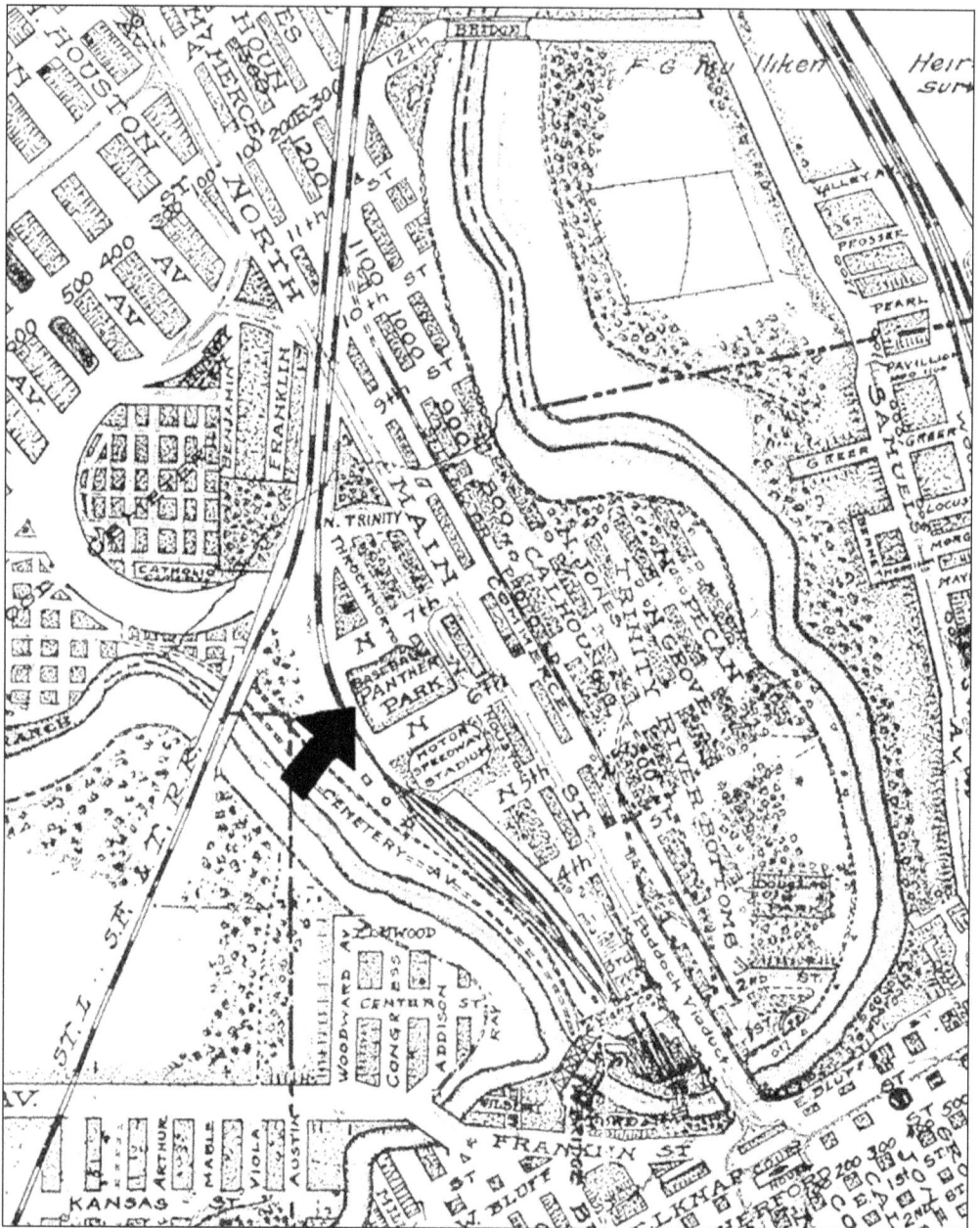

The new park completed for the 1911 season was originally named Morris Park and was located between North Sixth and North Seventh streets west of North Main. Interestingly, Panthers owner J. Walter Morris, for whom the new park was named, had played for and managed the San Antonio ball club and is still recognized as the only person to play, manage, own a team, and become president of the same minor league. The new park was originally built for a capacity of just over 4,000 but later additions would almost double that total. Panther Park also was the first to install turnstiles and have reserved seats, and Morris the first to incorporate the now popular "Rain Check" ticket. The electric rail system along Throckmorton Street would serve the field well and the workers of the North Fort Worth meat packing plants would have easier access to games. It was later named Panther Park when Morris sold his interests following the 1914 season.

Panther Park served as home to the famous Fort Worth teams of the 1920s that won six straight Texas League championships. It would host the first Dixie Series game matching the champion of the Southern Association with that of the Texas League and would also become the site of the first live radio broadcast in the South, when WBAP Radio aired the game against Wichita Falls on September 1, 1922. The park was built in an awkward configuration with the main grandstand along the first base line and little or no seating along the third base line. Later additions would add seating behind home plate and along the third base line toward North Main Street. In this photo several championship pennants can be seen in flying in centerfield.

The ownership group of W.K. Stripling and Paul LaGrave felt a new ballpark was needed following the league championship in 1925. A site was selected and the land purchased for a new concrete and steel structure to be built in the same general vicinity between 6th and 7th Streets, but this time on the east side of North Main tucked in against the Trinity River levy. This photo shows Paul LaGrave on the left and W.K. "Will" Stripling on the right sizing up their new purchase. The levy in the background has been maintained over the years to keep the Trinity River from flooding the area but could not stop the rains in 1949.

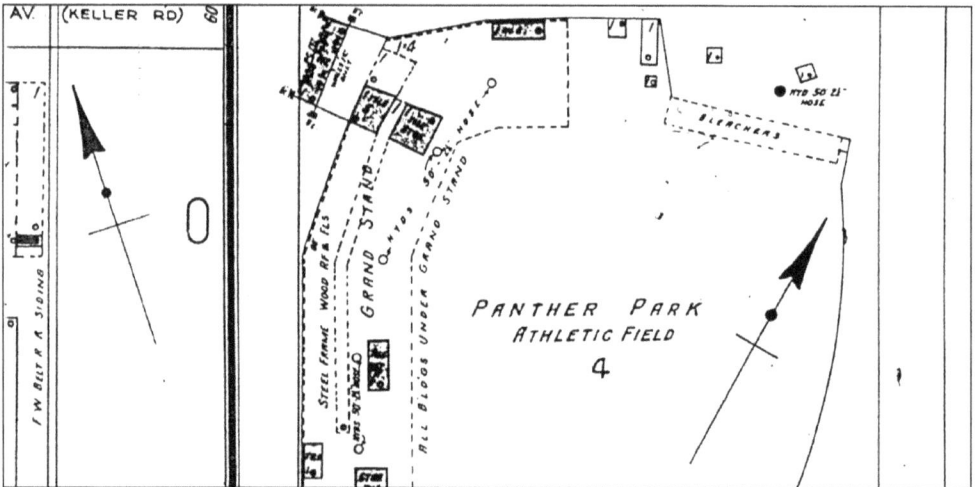

This was the configuration of Panther Park as it was built for the 1926 season. The seating capacity for the original park was listed at 12,000 with the roof and stands running only a short distance down the third base line, similar to the configuration of the west side Panther Park. In January of 1929 Paul LaGrave passed away after a long illness and W.K. Stripling honored his friend and business partner by renaming Panther Park as LaGrave Field. Despite an inauspicious beginning (the Panthers failed to win the Texas League crown for the first time in six years in the park's inaugural season), the site and the name have held special memories for thousands of fans for many years.

This photo from 1937 shows the field as it looked when Lou Gehrig and the New York Yankees visited LaGrave Field for an exhibition game against the Panthers. Many major league players and teams played their way through Fort Worth on their travels north from spring training. On the south side (bottom) of the right field bleachers was the home of Wortham Field, a football stadium serving the north side communities. Notice also the lack of seating down the left field and right field baselines. These sections were added later to bring the seating capacity to 12,415. A section of bleachers in right field also served as the seating area for black patrons prior to the integration of the ballpark.

In the early Sunday morning of May 15, 1949 the grandstands of LaGrave Field caught fire and were totally destroyed. That afternoon the San Antonio Missions were in town to play the Cats and 3,000 fans sat in temporary box seats to watch Joe Landrum and the Cats lose a 2-0 ballgame. The early newspaper reports considered arson but later investigation pointed to an electrical short. Manager Bobby Bragan and team president John Reeves were awakened that morning and had to watch as the field burned.

One day after the fire heavy rains hit Fort Worth and the Trinity River overflowed the levy behind left field and flooded the area. The fire caused an estimated one million dollars in damage to the park and almost cost Fort Worth their baseball team. The flood, however, caused an estimated 25 million dollars in damage to the city, forcing 13,000 from their homes. Branch Rickey and Walter O'Malley later flew to Fort Worth to assess the future of the franchise in city. The Cats moved the remainder of the home series with San Antonio to the Alamo city and Houston owner Allen Russell followed with an invitation to John Reeves to move the Cats scheduled home series with the Buffaloes to Houston and allow Fort Worth be the home team with the home share of the gate.

The Brooklyn Dodgers and Cats president John Reeves announced the field would be rebuilt in its current location. This was a great relief for the fans of Fort Worth as speculation spread that the Dodgers would not spend the money for a new facility. Herman G. Cox was hired as the architect and engineer and construction began shortly after the 1949 season. The capacity would be increased to 13,005 and for the first time in any ballpark, facilities for television would be designed and built into the press box structure. Other amenities included larger restrooms for the ladies, new concession stands fitted with a griddle, bun warmer, large drink containers, and new form fitting bucket style seats with arm rests. Total cost for the construction exceeded one million dollars. Compare the seat installations of this 1950 photo with the photo 52 years later when the new LaGrave Field was built.

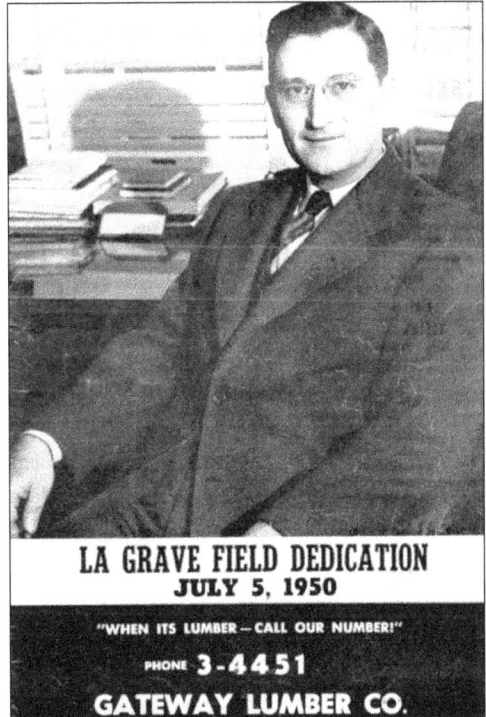

LA GRAVE FIELD DEDICATION
JULY 5, 1950

"WHEN ITS LUMBER — CALL OUR NUMBER!"

PHONE **3-4451**

GATEWAY LUMBER CO.

In a letter to Mrs. Paul LaGrave, Brooklyn Dodgers President Branch Rickey wrote, "It seemed to me to be proper to have the Fort Worth park remain known as LaGrave Field. All of us are proud of the park there and believe the people of Fort Worth will also be pleased with it." On July 5, 1950, the organization held a dedication of the new park for the fans. The day included a luncheon, a parade, the dedication ceremony, and a game with the Dallas Eagles. Fort Worth Mayor Edgar Deen, Brooklyn Dodgers executives Branch Rickey and Walter O'Malley, and thousands of fans were in attendance.

95

The right field bleacher section of LaGrave Field was not damaged by the 1949 fire. Paul LaGrave had always believed baseball was for kids and should be available to all youngsters. As far back as the old Panther Park a right field seating section existed with kids in mind. For many years kids could purchase a very inexpensive membership to the Knot Hole Gang. With their membership card they could enter this section of the ballpark card for any game during the season. Some years the team would give the cards away to kids that demonstrated straight A's or exemplary citizenship in school. When the new LaGrave Field was built in 2002, Carl Bell and his associates made sure the tradition of the right field seating area was continued.

This was the view in the mid-1950s that most fans would see when driving into the parking area at LaGrave. The top floor served as offices and the bottom as the ticket booths and main entrance. The large neon "Cats" was not a part of the first ticket office but added when the field was rebuilt in 1950.

Advertisers have always been a major part of the revenue production for minor league baseball. Without the sponsors and advertisers most minor league clubs would not be able to exist. Here, in this 1958 photo, the Falstaff beer company has a handy display under the stands in the concession area of LaGrave. When the field was rebuilt, several light fixtures like the one in the upper right-hand corner were found.

This 1955 photo shows the field without the right field pavilion, which was torn down in the winter of 1954 as it had fallen in disrepair. This is also the configuration of the field when it was demolished in the winter of 1967. Elmer Kosub, long time athletic director and coach at St. Mary's University in San Antonio, was instrumental in seeing that the field parts were put to good use. Bleacher sections ended up as seating for Marble Falls High School and the softball field at St. Mary's. The light standards were moved to the baseball field of Pan American University in Edinburg, Texas. Miller's Wrecking and Excavation Company was responsible for the teardown and by February only a vacant field was left.

Lon Goldstein Field served as the first home of the Cats when they returned from extinction in 2001. The field is primarily used for high school baseball but $250,000 in improvements brought the stadium up to minor league specifications. The improvements included new chairback seats, new outfield fence, new scoreboard, and other amenities in the pressbox to make it a great place to view the first-year team. The field was named in honor of Leslie Elmer "Lon" Goldstein, who after 15 years of professional baseball began a 38 year career with the Fort Worth School District.

The seating capacity for Goldstein Field was only 3,400 and that hindered the Opening Day crowd in 2001, which could easily have exceeded 5,000. Many improvements were needed to bring the ballpark to minor league standards. Additions included a 16-foot outfield fence, new lights, a new sound system, new scoreboard, and a replacement of thousands of bench seats with chair-back seating.

For years, a grassy lot surrounded by hackberry trees, buried concrete dugouts, and some old tiled areas was all that remained of what was once the jewel of minor league baseball. In 1992, during the Society of American Baseball Research's national convention, an optional tour was arranged at the site of the former LaGrave Field. Eighty-five attendees made the bus trip from Arlington and paid homage to the hallowed grounds. Also in attendance were several members of past Fort Worth Cat teams including Bob Austin from Panhandle, Texas, Homer Matney from Wichita Falls, and local residents Jack Lindsey, Joe Macko, Carroll Beringer, Mike Lemish, and Bobby Bragan. It would be the first congregation of Cats players to officially gather in LaGrave since 1964. It would also be the first time discussions to rebuild the park would take place.

Little dirt had to be excavated for the playing surface when effort got underway to rebuild LaGrave Field. Once the grass and weeds were removed the baselines were platted using a map of the old field with the dugouts as a point of reference. The intersection of the baselines was hopefully the exact location where home plate had once stood. This was verified when, 90 feet down each line from the intersection, the original base stakes that once held first and third base to their moorings were found still in the ground. The construction team took great care in preserving the original dugouts that are used today for special field level boxes.

Long time groundskeeper and current stadium contractor Jim Anglea and his staff managed the construction for LaGrave Field. The team had a little more than three months to complete the project. Working right up to the day of the park's opening game, Anglea's team was painting railings and adding amenities. As shown in this 2002 photo the construction techniques for seat placements have not changed in the 50 years since the last time LaGrave was originally built.

A ballpark in Fort Worth would not be complete without a right field pavilion. During the course of each season there are several group nights when thousands of kids in brightly covered t-shirts sit in the pavilion. During the first year of new park's existence this was the only covered area of the ballpark and during rain delays many sought shelter there, including the ball players in the bullpen.

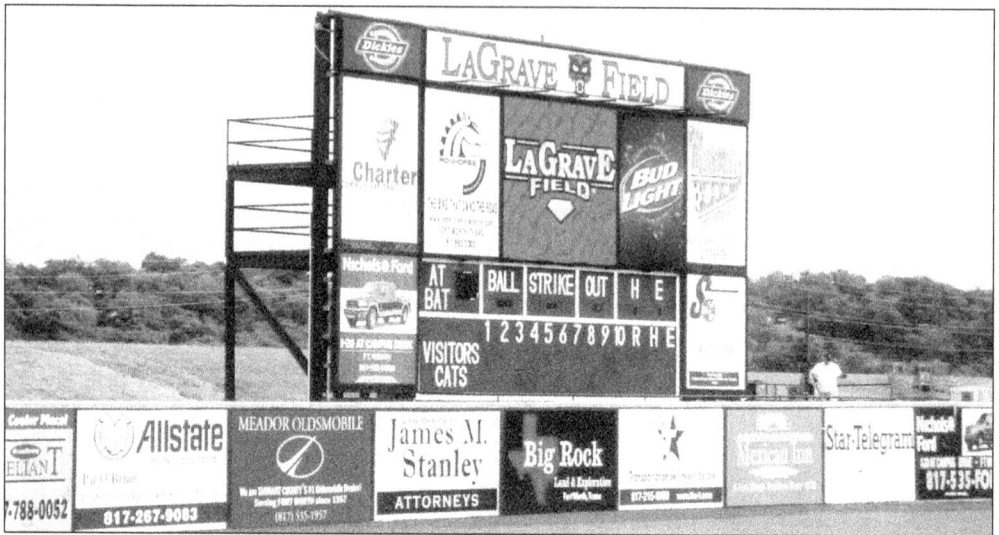

Combining eras, the new scoreboard at LaGrave features both an electronic video screen and a mechanical scoreboard. An attendant must hang the numbers to indicate runs, hits, and errors. This job offers the attendant a great view of the action on the field. A large bell was added to the scoreboard in 2003 and is the original bell given to Bobby Bragan's team in the early fifties. In 1951 the bell was rung to signal the start of the game. In 2003 the bell can be heard after a Cats player hits a home run. The video action is all controlled in the announcer's booth by Frankie Gasca and his team.

The last modification to the stadium was the completion of the roof over the reserved seat sections. The roof not only offers shade during a hot Texas summer but also protection from the late spring storms that often push through the area. The roof was designed so the location of no pole would result in an obstructed view of the field. Plans are in place for permanent locker and bathroom facilities behind each of the baselines and permanent concession areas on the concourse. There has also been discussion to build a baseball museum on or near the LaGrave Field property and dedicated to none other than Bobby Bragan.

SEVEN

The Negro Leagues in Fort Worth

During the late 1800s baseball was a growing pastime for many town teams. The Texas League, having been established in 1888, was the first all professional league in the state but town teams were playing one another all over Texas. Several area black colleges formed teams but the players were unable to continue their play in the established white professional leagues. As a result, African-Americans organized their own semi-pro and amateur leagues throughout Texas. The first indication of "colored" baseball in Fort Worth was a game being played in June of 1891. The *Fort Worth Gazette* described a championship series between Dallas and Fort Worth, which was to be played at the Fair Grounds Park. The roster of the team representing Fort Worth in that series was listed as: Wims, catcher; Itson, pitcher; Brockman, first base; Greer, second base; Smith, shortstop; Bateman, third base; Pratt in left field; Adams in center field and Carter in right field.

Discovering information about the early black teams is difficult at best. Many newspapers of the time failed to report on the black teams of the era and often small articles would reference upcoming games with no later account of the actual game. Many players were focused on playing for teams with which they could earn higher wages and thus jumped teams often at the prospect of more money. Teams would frequently pick up local players in the cities where they traveled in order to complete their rosters. Some of the locals played well enough to travel with the team and become permanent members while others would quickly become homesick and return home.

The most recognized local barnstorming teams included the Fort Worth Black Cats and the Mineola Black Spiders. The Black Cats even played an exhibition game in Fort Worth's LaGrave Field against the Negro American League Champion Cleveland Buckeyes in 1945.

The Depression forced the shutdown of many minor leagues throughout baseball and the Negro leagues were no exception. Nevertheless, the impact these teams had on local cities and towns was tremendous and it will never be fully appreciated. The teams offered a venue of entertainment for both black and white fans and the level of baseball play was often very high. It is hoped that with this book a little more recognition will be given to these players and owners and the contributions they made to baseball in Fort Worth.

ANDREW (RUBE) FOSTER

RATED FOREMOST MANAGER AND EXECUTIVE IN
HISTORY OF NEGRO LEAGUES. ACCLAIMED TOP
PITCHER IN BLACK BASEBALL FOR NEARLY A
DECADE IN EARLY 1900s. FORMED CHICAGO
AMERICAN GIANTS IN 1911 AND BUILT THEM
INTO MIDWEST'S DOMINANT BLACK TEAM. IN
1920 HE ORGANIZED NEGRO NATIONAL LEAGUE.
HEADED LEAGUE AND MANAGED CHICAGO TEAM
UNTIL RETIREMENT FOLLOWING 1926 SEASON·

The future of the professional Negro National League can trace its roots to a Texas colored league. Andrew "Rube" Foster, recognized as the founder of the Negro National League in 1920, played for a local Fort Worth team. Born in Calvert, Texas just southeast of Waco, Foster was 17 during the 1896 season when he played for the Fort Worth Yellowjackets. A 1902 article reporting on the "Fort Worth colored nine" exclaimed, "Foster, the local colored crack pitcher shut out the Waco team." The story goes on to describe how the Waco nine was considered the best in the state and that special seating was arranged for white patrons. Foster soon moved to the Chicago area where he became a businessman, played baseball, founded new teams, and eventually the new league. Historian John Holway noted in the spring of 1911 Foster brought his American (Leland) Giants to Fort Worth for spring training among much fanfare.

Black baseball at the turn of the century was primarily barnstorming tours with little in the way of organized schedules or rosters. This would eventually change with Foster's highly organized Negro National League. Fort Worth had several teams that barnstormed Texas and other states to play exhibitions for the gate receipts. The most famous team from Fort Worth was named the "Wonders." That club was formed in 1905, and the 1909 roster including such notables as sluggers George Washington "Dibo" Johnson and Louis "Big Bertha" Santop, seen here. Santop, born in San Antonio, is considered one of the greatest catchers of his time. Biz Mackey, who played briefly in Fort Worth in 1919, and Josh Gibson are more highly recognized for their catching and hitting talents in the established Negro Leagues but those who mention Santop do so in reverence. He was the first to be called the "Black Babe Ruth."

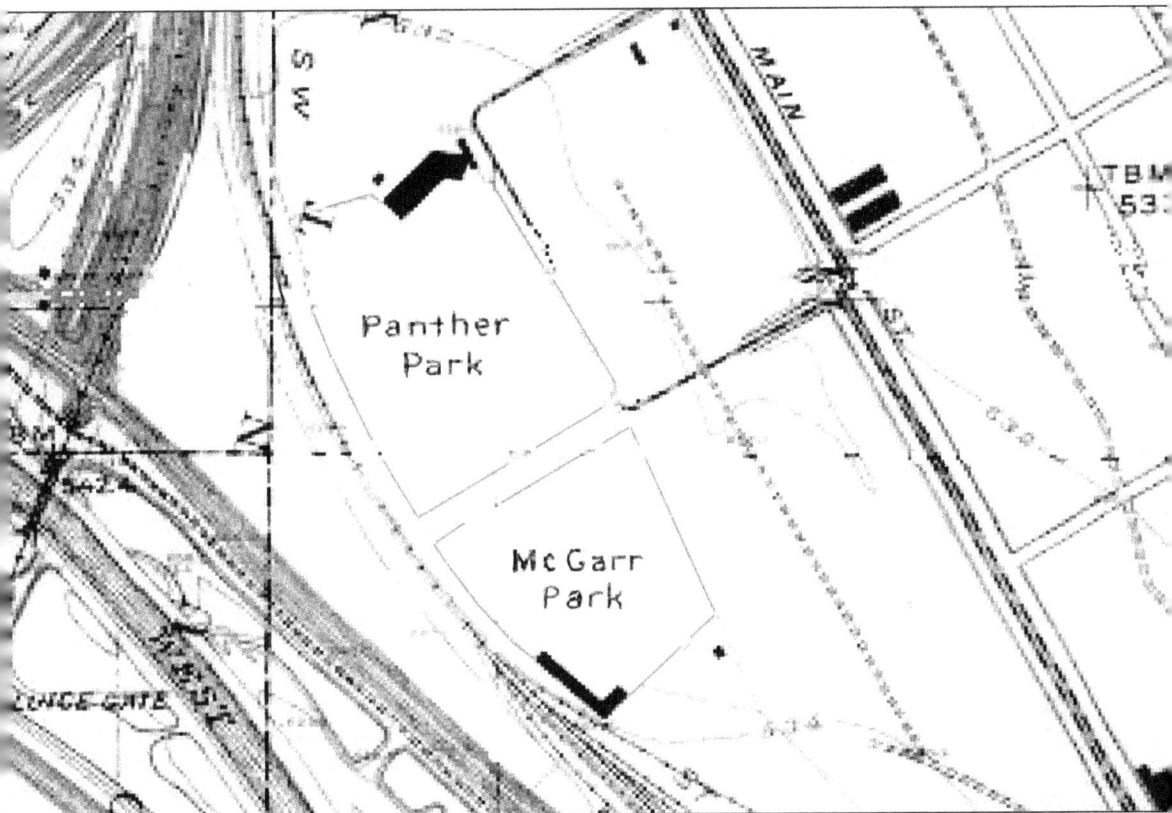

In 1916 Hiram McGar of Fort Worth served as President of the Colored Texas League. His team, the Fort Worth Black Panthers, played in McGar Park which was located just south of Panther Park's center field wall. The park would not survive long and would later become a motor raceway. There is a reference that the park "included special seating for white patrons." McGar was a local saloon and social club owner and a major force in the organization of the Texas Negro League in 1920. The teams included in the 1916 Colored Texas League were Cleburne, Dallas, Waco, Houston, San Antonio, Beaumont, and Galveston and the league played a schedule of 142 games.

Black Panthers Defeat San Antonio Bears Twice

TEXAS NEGRO LEAGUE.

Clubs—	Won.	Lost.	Pct.
Fort Worth	20	12	.625
Dallas	16	16	.500
Wichita Falls	14	18	.438
San Antonio	13	19	.406
Beaumont	12	20	.375
Houston	12	20	.375

The Fort Worth Black Panthers took a twin bill from the Santone Black Bears at Panther park 2 to 0 and 3 to 0. "Steel Arm" Johnny Harris applied the whitewash in the opener while Willie Harris duplicated in the last contest The features of the game was unique. W Jones, Fort Worth shortstopper, stole home while the visiting pitcher was winding up. The catcher never received the ball until the local duskie had safely hit the plate.

These two clubs will play again this afternoon at the Panther ball lot. Hudson will hurl for the Panthers Score.

The Texas Negro League was established in 1920 with the help of Hiram McGar, still operator of the Fort Worth club, and A.S. Wells of Dallas, who served as the league president. J.I. Dotson of Fort Worth served as the league secretary. These teams were completely professional and arrangements had been made to play in the Texas League parks when the Texas League "white" occupants were on the road. Marlin Carter, who played in the league during the late 1920s, believes the league was much better than "minor leagues" and as good as any major league. "Competition in the league was always tough. Some of the best black players at that time were down in Texas. It's hard to say that the teams in that league weren't as good as the teams that were playing in the Negro National League." (From an interview of Marlin Carter by P. Mills in *Black Ball News*). Hiram McGar, owner the Fort Worth Club, would also serve as its manager. Pitchers Cornelius Rector and Willie Harris, third baseman Johnson Hill, and catcher Spearman all played well for Fort Worth, as evidenced by the league standings seen here, and the result was a first place finish in 1920 for the Black Panthers.

Haines Pitches No-Hit Game for Black Panthers

Pitcher Haines of the Black Panthers pitched the first no-run, no-hit game to be staged in Panther park this season when he handed the package to the Black Spudders in the first game of a double-header yester-

Fort Worth a 1-to-0 victory.

In the second game the Black Spudders were victorious by a 3-to-2 score.

The third game of the series will be played this afternoon at 4:30 o'clock. Steel Arm will work for the Black Panthers and Hicks for the Black Spudders. Special reservations are made for white fans in the grandstand at all games.

Scores:

First game—

	R.	H.	E.
Black Panthers	000 000 001—1	2	0

The Texas-Oklahoma-Louisiana (TOL) League organized and was operated as a recognized black minor league from 1929 through 1932. Quincy J. Gilmore, former secretary for the Negro National League, called on several black leaders to form the league. They met at the Pythian Temple in Dallas in January of 1929 and it was decided that teams would be located in the same cities as the white Texas League with the exception of the Oklahoma teams (though those cities would soon join the Texas League). Teams were located in Shreveport, Dallas, Houston, Tulsa, San Antonio, Oklahoma City, Wichita Falls, and Fort Worth. William Tresivant of Fort Worth, who founded what eventually became the city's Colored Country Club, was elected commissioner and Gilmore served as the league president. Mr. English was chosen as the Black Panthers first manager but would be replaced on July 11th by Ruben Jones. Jones had a long history as a manager in the Negro leagues and former Negro league player William Blair once said, "the man hated to lose." Jesse Haines, as seen in a newspaper clipping here, threw what would be the only no-hitter of that first season at Panther Park in 1929. Some of the players listed in the scarce box scores of the era included pitchers Shaw, Hancock, and Pervin with catchers Roberts and Robinson. It was recorded that almost 6,000 fans witnessed a two-game series between Fort Worth and Dallas in Dallas.

The Cats integrated the field house in the late thirties with the hiring of long time clubhouse man Alex Thomas. Carl Erskine once wrote that Thomas made an ointment for pitchers that was the most "penetratenest" stuff in existence. Alex served the Cats until the 1958 season when he moved to Shreveport. Not enough is known about Mr. Thomas but his service to the Cats' players is recognized by all who knew him.

Local baseball icon Marion "Jap" Jones, seen here in a recent photo, remembers an exhibition game arranged between the House of David barnstorming troupe and a team of local black All-Stars. He was attending summer school at Wiley College and was asked to play for the All-Star squad with the promise of a check for doing so. Jones played the game, which was held in mid-summer of 1951 at LaGrave Field, but only saw half of what he was promised. "Sonny" Smith, who played for the Chicago American Giants from 1948 through 1950, said they would often barnstorm through Fort Worth, playing games against a local All-Star team. "They weren't usually very 'All-Star' in talent though," he said. Smith also noted the games in which he played were not held at LaGrave Field but usually at a city or high school park.

Two Negro Players Sent Cats by Parent Dodgers

Dolan Sold, Stankey Optioned To Elmira in Roster Shuffling

STOP, THIEF!—Cats' Danny Ozark is thrown out stealing on first game of doubleheader with Houston Sunday at La Grave Field. Making catch is Houston's Stanton Bruan. Crossing to cover Ozark is Alan Grandcolas.

Alertness Pays For Eagle Nine

4 Games in 5 Days for TCU

SPORTS IN BRIEF

Missions Tall in Saddle As TL Leaders Break Ev-

The 1950s was an important decade for black baseball in Fort Worth. Dave Hoskins broke the color barrier in the Texas League when he signed with the Dallas Eagles in 1952 and black players began to appear at Fort Worth Cats games as members of visiting teams. The Cats themselves remained an all-white institution for three more seasons. That all changed in 1955 when the Dodgers sent Maury Wills and Eddie Moore to Fort Worth, thus integrating the team. Wills, who stayed in a loft apartment above the train station in downtown, says his stay in Fort Worth was enjoyable and it allowed him to play for Bobby Bragan, whom he credits with getting him to the majors. With the integration of the team, LaGrave Field, which at one time only included a special seating area for "colored" patrons, was soon completely opened to all fans.

SHREVEPORT BASEBALL CLUB

BLEACHER - COLORED ADULT..........75c

Admission.........73   State Tax.........02

NOT GOOD IF DETACHED-Good Date Sold Only

Management reserves right to revoke license granted by ticket by refunding purchase price.

84 166057

Special arrangements had to be made for teams traveling to Shreveport, Louisiana, as the city would not allow black players to play on white teams. The Texas League gave special roster exemptions to allow teams to add two white players to their rosters when traveling to Shreveport. Most teams did allow black patrons to attend the games but only in special seating areas. In 1958 Fort Worth slugger Joe Macko was picked up by the Corpus Christi Giants to play Birmingham in the Dixie Series. The series was almost postponed because black players were not allowed to play in Birmingham but the two black players on the Corpus Christi roster were injured and not going to make the trip. To avoid any further tensions the team picked up Macko and another white player, Art Dunham of Dallas, for the series.

108

The amateur baseball ranks were still very segregated during 1950s. Negro amateur leagues were established with teams all over Texas. The league champions would meet in a state championship tournament and for many years the event was held in Waco, but in May of 1953, a tornado swept through Katy Park and forced a cancellation of the event. Not to be deterred, Marion Jones moved the championship to Fort Worth for the Labor Day weekend. The Harmon Field League sponsored the championships and the games were played at Rockwood Park. This photo is from the Jaxx team that played in the amateur leagues of the late '50s. Rayford Maddox, seated front row on the right, was the manager and organizer of the team, helping Marion Jones with league responsibilities as well. Black high schools did not play baseball until 1953 when Jones started the first high school baseball team at I.M Terrell High School and the first high school baseball district with Dallas schools Booker T. Washington and Lincoln High. There were no fields or a sponsor for the games but turnout was positive and well accepted by the kids. Finally, in 1966, the state of Texas mandated the integration of high school athletics. Though integration of the amateur ranks was still several years away the door was opened for equal opportunity for all ball players.

Every season the Cats franchise has made an effort to recognize the contributions the Negro Leagues made to our National Pastime. The Cats celebrate Negro League night by wearing uniforms representing former Fort Worth Negro teams the Wonders, Black Panthers, and Black Cats. John "Mule" Miles, who played from 1946 through 1948 with the Chicago American Giants, was a guest of the Cats in 2003 and is seen here posing with Cats manager Wayne Terwilliger. A native of San Antonio, Miles was given the nickname "Mule" for his power at the plate when he hit 26 homeruns in 1946.

Mel Hall played thirteen years of major league baseball with the Chicago Cubs, Cleveland Indians, New York Yankees, and San Francisco Giants. Hall hit for a .276 lifetime average that included 134 big league home runs. He returned from a five-year retirement to play and coach for the Cats in 2002. Hall batted .300 for the Cats before being released and signing with the Springfield/Ozark Mountain Ducks. Though he never had to play in the segregated Negro Leagues he posed here in the unofficial uniform of the Fort Worth Black Cats during the an annual tribute the Cats club holds each year to honor the Negro League history of Fort Worth. Hall makes Fort Worth his home in the off-season and works with kids to help develop their baseball talents.

110

EIGHT

The Panther Returns

2001–Present

For the last 40 years the empty lot on the east side of North Main Street went unnoticed. If you would have walked onto the open field at the corner of NE 6th and Calhoun Streets you would have been surrounded by trees in the shape of a baseball diamond. The concrete dugouts that once served as benches for Duke Snider, Sparky Anderson, Maury Wills, and Rogers Hornsby were still there and the right field concrete footers where the outfield fence once stood could be found. Behind each of the dugouts were areas of tiled floors that were once showers and locker rooms and if you stood on the spot where you thought home plate might have been you could only have imagined what it must have looked like during the heyday of the Cats.

In 1994 the Society of American Baseball Research held their national convention in Arlington, Texas. A reunion and tour of former LaGrave Field was organized as part of the festivities. Eighty-five people and eight former Cats attended a wonderful meeting of ballplayers and fans at the site of so many historic Texas League games. This momentum generated the interests of several city leaders including Joe Dulle and city councilman Jim Lane. They, with the involvement of Texas Wesleyan University and the city of Fort Worth, began the idea to return baseball to the north side. After several years of discussions and planning, Carl Bell and the ownership group that became Texas Independent Baseball, LLC delivered to Fort Worth a plan, a strategy, and most importantly the passion to bring the Cats back to life.

The All-American Association, a new independent minor league, was formed with member cities throughout the southeastern states. A Fort Worth franchise became a member and the passion for minor league baseball soon began anew in a converted high school field on the city's south side. On June 7, 2001, the Cats officially returned professional baseball to Fort Worth. A year later, with several All-American teams in financial instability, the ownership group negotiated a membership in the former Texas Louisiana League and became a member of the newly named Central League of Professional Baseball. More importantly Bell and his associates set their sites on building a new baseball facility on the exact site of the former LaGrave Field that was to be ready for play in 2002. The field has been recognized as the best playing field in the Central League for two straight years and by the end of the 2003 season the Cats brought playoff baseball back to Fort Worth.

The partnership known as Texas Independent Baseball was the catalyst for bringing the professional game back to Fort Worth. The group represented by Dan Fergus, Scott Berry, Gary Elliston, Pete O'Brien, Michael Halbrooks, and Chairman Carl Bell joined Cliff Wall, absent from this picture, to bring a structure and management team to the Fort Worth franchise. Former major league first baseman Pete O'Brien also served as the Cats Director of Player Personnel, finding the baseball talent for the Cats.

Carl Bell fondly remembers when his family would make the two-hour drive north from Waco to attend a Fort Worth Cats game and says his father was the influence for his love of baseball. "We would sit in general admission behind the first base line and I became an instant Fort Worth Cats fan," he recalled. It was his dream and ambition to bring that fun and excitement back to Fort Worth for another generation of fans to revel in the excitement of minor league baseball. Through the efforts of Bell and the Texas Independent Baseball group, minor league baseball has prospered on the north side of Fort Worth.

The site chosen for the first-year team was a high school baseball field on the city's south side. The field was named Lon Goldstein Field in honor of the former major league baseball player and city athletic director. (Goldstein played parts of two seasons with the Cincinnati Reds.) Located at Interstate 20 and Wichita Street in south Fort Worth the field only served the new Cats for their first year. This view from the left field bullpen shows the quaint size of the ballpark and the 30-foot monster chain link fence separating the stands from the field. Temporary bleachers were brought in and placed down each line to bring the total capacity to about 3,400 seats.

A great enjoyment for any fan is Opening Day and the new beginning it represents. Former ballplayers who once graced the field for their own home openers also enjoy the chance to return, be recognized for their contributions, and become part of the festivities. The Fort Worth Cats ownership and management team have always recognized the history of the Fort Worth Cats franchise and the players that made it special. Since many chose to make Fort Worth their home it was easy to organize a special luncheon for former Cats Carroll Beringer, Mike Napoli, Eldon Hill, Jack Lindsey, Joe Macko, and Walter Butler, who all gathered to share their memories at one of Fort Worth's historic eating establishments, Joe T. Garcia's.

The Opening Day festivities on June 7, 2001, included clowns, a flyover by vintage airplanes, and the National Anthem sung by the Broadway Baptist Church Chapel Choir. Before the game a Dixieland band played long and loud in front of the stadium. The ball club had to endure not having enough seating for the overflow crowd and having an electrical fuse fail, rendering the loud speakers and scoreboard useless. It didn't matter to the crowd of 3,056, who saw professional baseball for the first time in Fort Worth since 1964. Bobby Bragan was appropriately chosen to toss the first pitch and District 8 City Councilman Ralph McCloud chosen to receive it. McCloud was appropriately attired in a Brooklyn Dodger uniform top. The team won a 7-2 victory over the visiting Tennessee T's.

"Stray Cat," the first mascot of the ball club, was always well received because of the energy and creativity of Pat Fulps. Fulps also held the position as a marketing and sales representative for the new franchise but it was his on-field antics that entertained fans. In a game with the Baton Rouge Blue Marlins, "Stray" entered the field in front of the Baton Rouge bench dressed complete with fishing hat, vest, and pole. After throwing a line toward the bench he hooked a big one as an associate threw a stuffed toy Marlin over the dugout onto which "Stray" began to pounce as only a true Cat would.

Another focus of the Cats is the Field of Dreams program for youth teams. Youth teams from throughout the area may schedule a day with the Cats, with each member of the team escorting the starting nine of the Cats to their positions. The kids then stand for the "National Anthem" before exiting. Here one of the Cats players is signing autographs for the youth players before he takes the field.

This 2001 squad was the first team to return professional baseball to Fort Worth. The group included former major league players Jim Gentile as their manager and pitcher Jose Guzman as their ace. The team also included many local players who played high school baseball in the Fort Worth or Dallas area and went on to successful college or minor league careers. These included Mark Austry, Pat Hannon, brothers Chris and Kyle Houser, Bobby McIntire, Clint Davis, Tapley Holland, and Flint Wallace. The team managed a 37-35 record, good for fourth place and a first round playoff series with the first-place Baton Rouge club. Baton Rouge won the series and the league championship with a second round series win over the Albany Alligators.

Former major league and Cats first baseman Jim Gentile returned to Fort Worth as the team's first manager in 2001 and managed for most of the 2002 season. Gentile was a three time American League All-Star from 1960 to 1962 and spent seven and a half years in the major leagues. He played first base for the Brooklyn Dodgers, Baltimore Orioles, Kansas City Athletics, and Houston Astros between 1956 and 1965. During his major league career he pounded 180 homeruns and hit another 240 as a minor leaguer. In Gentile's first year with the Cats the team qualified for the playoffs with a fourth-place finish in the All-American Association.

A fan favorite for the first two years of the franchise, Jackie Davidson served as both pitcher and pitching coach in his two year stint with the Cats. A Fort Worth area native, Davidson became a two-time All-State selection at Everman High School and the sixth overall pick in the June 1983 major league draft. He spent six years in the Chicago Cubs organization. During his first year with the Cats, Davidson posted six wins against three losses and struck out 36 batters in 48 innings.

It was like old times when Carroll Beringer threw to his former catcher Mike Napoli while former Cats infielder Jack Lindsey grabbed a bat. The three were touring the former and future site of LaGrave Field when someone donned a bat, ball, and glove. As kids will be the group could not wait to begin play. The site would soon be covered with bulldozers and other heavy machinery moving dirt to begin the transformation to a ballpark.

On December 3, 2001, the Fort Worth organization officially broke ground for the new stadium. Seven former Cats attended the official groundbreaking ceremonies. Garbed in uniform tops from the current team were Joe Macko, Moe Santomauro, Carroll Beringer, Mike Napoli, Jack Lindsey, Bobby Bragan, Jim Gentile, and former business and general manager L.D. Lewis. The group is seen sitting in the former first base dugout that has been refurbished in the new stadium and which now serves Cats fans as a luxury box available for rent during game days.

Taking the mound in front of 5,619 fans on Opening Day of May 23, 2002, was pitcher Jose Guzman, seen here on the mound. This was the first professional game to be played on the original site of LaGrave Field since September of 1964. Except for some long lines at the concession area, the new ballpark offered the fans a great venue for summertime fun. The staff, led by general manager Monty Clegg, works overtime to make sure the fans have an entertaining evening at LaGrave Field. The on-field promotions and the off-field business needs are met by a great effort from a dedicated front office team.

The 2002 team featured many local players and included Shane Davenport, Mel Hall, Pat Hannon, Steve Hahn, Shawn Morgan, and Shawn Greene. Tony Jaramillo, nephew of Rangers hitting coach Rudy Jaramillo, and Foy Shemwell were the middle infielders. Six-foot-nine-inch Rick Powalski and Jose Guzman were the mound aces with Tyler Swinburnson, Matt Thomas, Shawn Onley, and Billy Coleman contributing to the pitching duties. Manager Jim Gentile had to resign in midseason to be with his wife and Marty Scott was asked to finish the year as manager. Former Rangers slugger Pete O'Brien donned a uniform again as one of his coaches. The team was now in the newly formed Central Baseball League, which featured teams from Edinburgh, Rio Grande (Harlingen), Springfield, MO; Alexandria, LA; Jackson, MS; Amarillo and San Angelo. The Cats finished out of contention for a playoff position but made a great run late in the season.

120

The only Cats player to play all three seasons since their return was outfielder Pat Hannon. A former All-American at Texas Wesleyan University in Fort Worth, Hannon finished the 2001 season as the Cats' Co-Player of the Year. He was second in the All-American Association batting race with a .340 batting average. Hannon made the decision to retire in July of 2003 to prepare for life after baseball. He accepted a coaching and teaching position in a local school district and married his fiancé who was also a former Texas Wesleyan All-American (volleyball). Leighann and Pat will always be a part of the Cats family and he will forever be recognized as the first player to hit a home run in the new LaGrave Field.

It is special in minor league baseball when the manager can find former major league players that have local appeal and can draw fans. When the player excels on the field then magic occurs. Such was the case when the Cats signed former Texas Rangers and Chicago Cubs pitcher Jose Guzman. Guzman's performances for the first-year Cats were outstanding. During the 2001 season he maintained a 1.65 earned run average and won five times in nine games. In 2002 he continued as the staff ace and in his final appearance on August 28, 2002, "Guzzie" pitched a five-hitter and beat the Amarillo Dillas for his last win as a professional. Guzman survived a tough childhood in Puerto Rico before signing with the Texas Rangers at the age of seventeen. One of the driving forces for "Guzzie" to continue his career in the independent leagues was a chance to let his children watch him pitch.

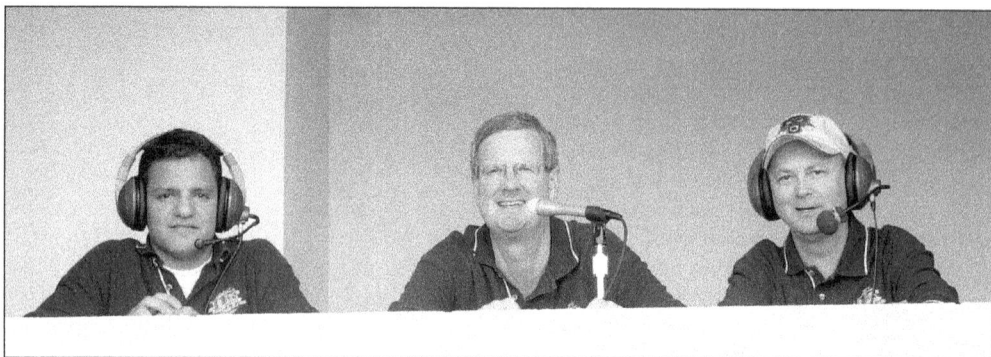

Radio is so much a part of the minor league baseball environment and in the great traditions of Bill Hightower and Tee Casper the current radio team, seen here from left to right, of Emil Moffatt, David Hatchett, and John Nelson have done an outstanding job of bringing the games into the cars and homes of fans who could not make it to the park. They carry on the great tradition of former Cats broadcasters that included those mentioned in earlier chapters and former Dallas Mayor Wes Wise. Cats games are currently broadcast on KTFW radio but it was KFJZ radio that carried the games in the late fifties and early sixties. The radio station even erected a sign in left field that carried the "KFJZ" letters and when a Cats player would step into the batter's box the number of letters corresponding to the number of hits for that player would light up. When a player reached four hits lighting up all four letters, the radio station would award that player a $25.00 check.

Fort Worth's baseball attention was shifted briefly when the Westside Lions Little League All-Stars traveled to Williamsport, Pennsylvania for the Little League World Series. The Westside All-Stars were the first Fort Worth area team to make the trip to Williamsport in forty-two years. The national television and newspaper coverage of the team's exploits brought an added excitement to the summer. Though the team was not able to win the championship they were recognized on August 28, 2002, as a season-high 7,219 fans crowded into LaGrave Field to honor the accomplishments of the future Cats.

Through a nomination by the office staff and a vote of the fans the name "Dodger" was given to the new mascot of the Fort Worth Cats. Dodger's presence is requested at many activities on and off the field. Children flock to Dodger for pictures and a handshake and he also makes time for a few crazed adults. A daily ritual for Dodger is to race a youngster chosen at random in a race around the base paths. He has raced over 150 times but has yet to win a single race.

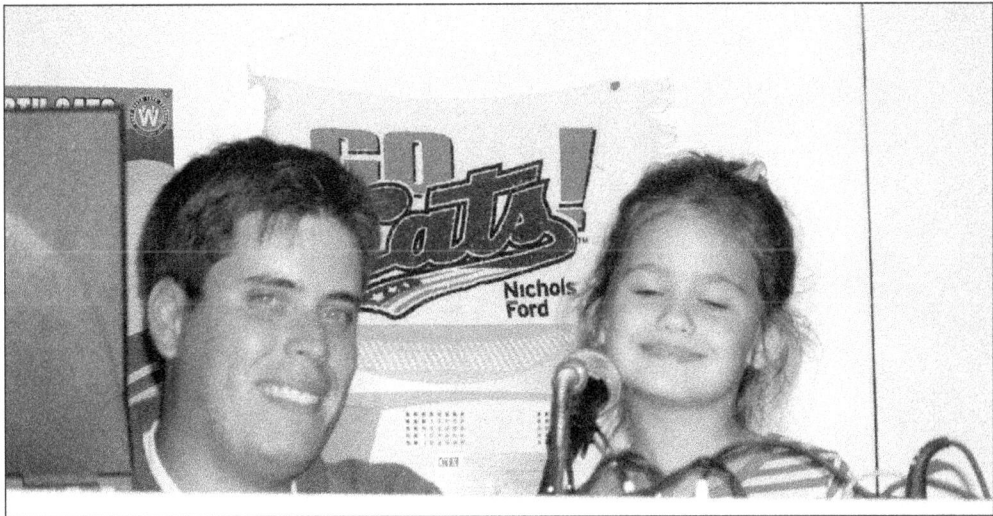

For three seasons the voice emanating from the loud speakers has been that of Frankie Gasca. First a student and now a high school baseball coach and teacher Frankie has served the Cats as their public address announcer since the beginning. Older fans might remember the voices of Gordon Fitzgerald, Charlie Gibson, or Jerry Hahn whose energies were heard over loudspeakers of the past. The announcers in minor league baseball can bring a personality to the on-field promotions and a connection between the game and the fans. In this photo Frankie is participating in another youth promotion helping a "guest" announcer with the Cats' line-up.

The first jersey retired in the history of the Cats fittingly belonged to Bobby Bragan. On May 24th the Cats front office presented Bobby with a framed jersey to hang in his office. Another representation of a jersey will forever hang on the right field pavilion. Bragan will hopefully soon be honored with the building of a baseball museum as part of the LaGrave Field complex dedicated to Bobby and home to his personal collection of baseball memorabilia.

For the 2003 season Barry Moss was named as the director of player personnel and he used his network of contacts to bring in players from throughout the country. Jim Essian, Bryon Smith, Brian Moon, Eric Mejas, and Ricky Gomez joined locals Hannon, Greene, Mark Hickey, and James Carroll on the roster. Matt Harrington returned after signing late in the 2002 season and, with Jermain Van Buren and Angel Aragorn, helped pitch the Cats to their first playoff appearance in the Central Baseball League. The team played the Jackson Senators in the first round playoff series. After splitting the first two games in Jackson the playoffs returned to Fort Worth where the Cats lost to the eventual league champions by a 2-1 score in an exciting fifth game.

Fan favorite Shawn Greene was voted the Central Baseball League's Player of the Month for June 2003 and has been with the team since 2002, when he was voted the Cats Co-MVP. Greene hit for a .270 average with 13 home runs in 2003 and pounded a crucial three-run homer in the sixth inning of a game with Rio Grande that helped the Cats clinch their playoff position. The 2003 season was his last in professional baseball before leaving to attend school to become a police officer. Shawn played in the Texas-Louisiana and Central Leagues for three seasons after graduating from Texas Wesleyan University.

The Texas heat can at times be stifling. Because of the heat many former Cats' pitchers described Fort Worth as a place where "it only took a few throws to warm up." With fan comfort foremost on their minds, Carl Bell and the Cats constructed a roof over the grandstand for the 2003 season. The original LaGrave Field's design had roof columns in the seating area but the new LaGrave's cantilever design allows for the columns to be situated behind the seating bowl, thus not obstructing anyone's view of the action. Fans sitting in the front row seats must now be alert for foul balls that have occasionally ricocheted off the front facing of the roof.

The recognition of Fort Worth as a great baseball town and a great baseball market has enabled the team to attract some very high profile talent for managers and coaches. Wayne "Twig" Terwilliger and Toby Harrah, along with pitching coach Dan Smith, made up the 2003 coaching staff. Terwilliger was recognized as the oldest manager in professional baseball when on his birthday of June 27th he was managing the Cats at the young age of 78. His playing career included eight years of major league service with the Cubs, Dodgers, Senators, Giants and Kansas City Athletics. Toby Harrah spent 17 years in the big leagues with the Senators, Rangers, Indians, and the Yankees. Harrah earned the honor as the fledgling Texas Rangers' first All-Star selection and he managed the Texas Rangers for a brief period before gaining the position of bench coach for the Colorado Rockies. Dan Smith, the third member of the staff, is also a former major league pitcher and the threesome led the 2003 Cats to a second half championship and the playoffs.

A special treat for Cats fans continues to be the return of former Cats ballplayers who are recognized for their contributions to the team's history. George "Sparky" Anderson returned in July of 2003 to throw out the first pitch, sit in the dugout with the team and sign autographs for the fans. The Cats also offered a special giveaway that featured Sparky as a bobblehead doll.

Maury Wills has done much for the Cats organization and he was hired as a vice president of special projects for the 2003 season. Wills has returned several times to Fort Worth to sign autographs, throw out the first pitch, and help the Cats players with their base running techniques. Here the former Dodgers star is shown signing autographs for the fans on the main concourse (prior to the roof construction).

"The Cats are Back, The Cats are Back" are part of the lyrics from the Cats first theme song, written and performed by musician Kim O'Connor. The singing cowboy, who can be found in the stands at many home games, is shown here singing the National Anthem. O'Connor has been performing professionally for over 30 years, singing throughout the United States and around the world. He has recorded ten CDs of original compositions, traditional western standards, railroad classics, Gospel, and Christmas favorites.

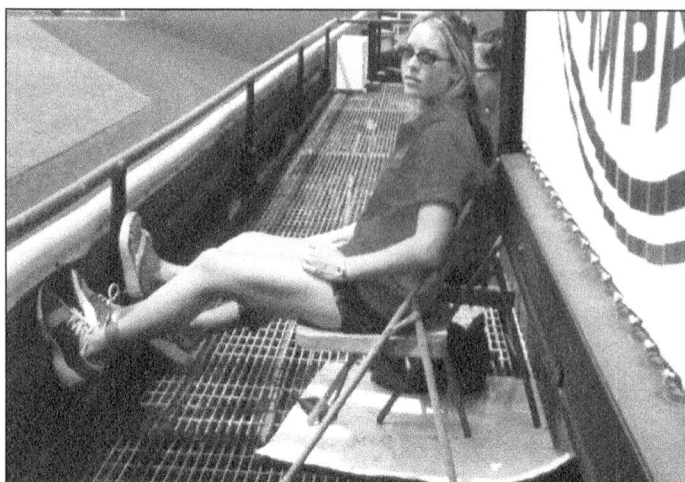

Minor league baseball is truly a family affair. For author Mark Presswood it goes a step beyond just attending the games with his family. His daughter Aly (*top*) works for the organization as the official keeper of the mechanical scoreboard and his youngest son Bret (*center*) occasionally takes his turn helping big sister with hanging the numbers. His oldest son Trey (*bottom*) served as the team's bullpen catcher for the first two years. Warming up pitchers who throw 90 mile-an-hour fastballs helped prepare Trey to continue his playing career in college. Mark's wife must not be forgotten, she is still the computer and internet consultant for the Cats and with her added responsibility of part-time photographer has thoroughly enjoyed her service with the Cats.

Visit us at
arcadiapublishing.com